UNSAFE AS HOUSES

UNSAFE AS HOUSES

A Guide to Home Safety

Neil Ewart

BLANDFORD PRESS
Poole   Dorset

First published in the U.K. 1981
by Blandford Press
Link House, West Street,
Poole, Dorset, BH15 1LL
Copyright © 1981 Blandford Books Ltd

British Library Cataloguing in Publication Data

Ewart, Neil
  Unsafe as houses.
  1. Home accidents – Prevention – Handbooks,
    manuals, etc.
  I. Title
614.8′53   TX150

ISBN 0 7137 1090 X

Printed in Great Britain by
Butler & Tanner Ltd,
Frome and London

CONTENTS

Contents

FIRST AID INDEX

First Aid Index

ACKNOWLEDGEMENTS

The author would like to express his thanks to the following organisations for their enthusiastic help during the research for this book.

The Fire Brigade. Fire Research Station. Fire Protection Association. British Safety Council. Health Education Council. The Home Accident Surveillance System and Consumer Safety Unit of the Department of Trade. The Royal Society for the Prevention of Accidents. The Royal Life Saving Society. The Medical Commission on Accident Prevention. The Pharmaceutical Society of Great Britain. The Electricity Council. Electrical Association for Women. British Gas Corporation. British Standards Institution. Safer Glazing Information Service. Age Concern. Disabled Living Foundation. British Aerosol Manufacturers' Association. Firework Makers' Guild. HM Coastguard. St John Ambulance Association. St Andrew's Ambulance Association. Red Cross Society.

I

A CHAPTER OF ACCIDENTS

When someone goes out of their house they are often told to 'take care'—whereas they should, in fact, be telling those who remain behind to do so. For more people die from accidents in the home than are killed on the roads or at work each year—with probably ten times as many being seriously injured.

Accidents happen not only in old or untidy houses, they happen even in the best-regulated households—and there are not just a dozen ways that we, our children, relatives, friends or visitors can be killed or injured—there are hundreds, with hazards where we least expect them.

This is a world-wide problem, whether we live in America, Australia or in Europe. In Great Britain alone, thousands of people die each year as a result of accidents in their homes. Hundreds of thousands more are injured, requiring hospital treatment, with many of the seriously injured being admitted as in-patients, taking up valuable bed space and resources in already over-crowded and overworked hospitals. It is estimated that at least 21 million people also require first aid due to accidents in the home.

Ask anyone which hazard they think is responsible for the most deaths in the home and almost all will say FIRE. This is certainly the most frightening—but the biggest danger is from FALLS. Though less spectacular and, therefore, receiving less publicity than fires—falls do more than injure, they are the biggest killer. What is more, falls are not necessarily from heights, a great many accidents are caused by falls at the same level.

POISONING is high on the list. Apart from medicines, many household substances and chemicals, and things growing in the garden, have poisoned adults and children, children in particular. Food poisoning is another common hazard. In some cases it merely causes discomfort—but in other cases it causes prolonged suffering which leads to death.

SUFFOCATION and CHOKING, ELECTROCUTION, BURNS and SCALDS all take their toll—with GLASS-RELATED ACCIDENTS seriously injuring tens of thousands of people, many being scarred or handicapped for life. Tragic accidents, some fatal, are caused by children and adults running, walking, or falling through glass doors, windows or partitions.

No one likes Mondays, and this is the day the highest number of accidents occur in the home. We need to be on our guard and take safety precautions every day, of course, but the total number of accidents rises to a peak again at weekends. With the changing social patterns and a shorter working week, greater leisure and more time spent at home— things could get worse. So we need to be more alert than ever to avoid becoming an accident victim or putting others at risk.

In densely populated areas, it is almost impossible to get through a day or night without hearing the siren from an ambulance or fire engine. Next time you hear one, do not just feel sorry for the victim, remind yourself that at some time in the future they *could* be coming to *your* home.

The purpose of this book is to prevent that. Accidents can happen to anyone, that's the bad news, the good news is that, if you follow the 'Safety in the Home' rules, unnecessary accidents can be prevented.

The safety advice in this book has been designed to help everyone. It will help parents, who buy appliances and furnishings and organise the daily running of the home; and it is hoped that the parents will pass the tips on to their children—many of whom will be the parents of tomorrow. It will help home and flat owners, tenants, and bedsitter dwellers, people of all ages—the elderly and the disabled—single adults and those living alone. All the information they need to know has been collected into *one* book.

The book does not tell you what to do or not to do without giving the reason and explaining why. Mentioning that may seem superfluous but, very often, such dangers as falls or fires are dismissed with advice to, 'make sure your stairs are well lit and don't leave objects around on them' or 'be sure to have a hose and fire extinguisher handy'.

The chapters which follow give the fullest coverage of every possible hazard, including many that are seldom mentioned, showing:

1 The various dangers and how the different accidents happen.
2 How to avoid and eliminate each hazard and make homes safe for everyone, including children, guests and visitors.
3 What to do if accidents happen, the emergency action which should be taken, and the first aid necessary.

This book has easy-to-find sections on the correct first aid treatment in each case of accident, as well as advice on purchasing or making up first aid kits and what they should contain.

The word '*Home*' is used in the widest sense, covering the garden and its ornamental pool, and the workshop and garage where so many accidents occur. *Home is home*, whether it is your full-time address or a hotel, caravan or tent when on holiday. Remember that while on holiday the seaside or countryside becomes your garden. Added safety precautions are given for the things, so often overlooked, which can easily turn a holiday into a tragedy.

When first aid is required it is needed in a hurry. In case of drowning, choking, or severe electric shock and other cases where the victim has ceased breathing, there are only *four minutes* in which to save a life— after that the brain is irreparably damaged.

Prompt first aid treatment while waiting for an ambulance and medical help to arrive, and knowing what to do and doing it correctly, can save lives. It can also prevent a minor injury from becoming a major one.

However, as *prevention is better than cure*, the aim of this book is to prevent accidents from happening in the first place.

2

FIRE

SMOKE—THE REAL KILLER

Fires are probably the most terrifying of all accidents in the home. People imagine that the smoke is harmless and that the flames are the main danger, but 80% of the people who die in fires often have no burn marks on them. They are killed by the toxic inhalation of smoke and fumes long before the flames ever touch them.

FOAM FURNITURE FIRES

Fires are caused for a variety of reasons—just think about the furniture in your home for a moment. If the fillings contain plastic materials, such as polyurethane or latex foam, you could be sitting on a time bomb! In Britain at least 1,000 people have died from foam furniture fires during the past ten years, and people are being killed at the rate of two a week. When polyurethane foam catches fire, whether in cushions, chairs, settees or mattresses, it gives off a dense black smoke and toxic gases that can kill within minutes.

The density of the fumes and speed at which they spread are frightening, and you do not have to be in the room where the fire started to be killed. The poisonous fumes spread everywhere, into the hall, upstairs and into bedrooms where many people, adults and children, have died without realising there was a fire below.

Visibility can be reduced to almost nil in no time at all, with carbon monoxide and other poisonous gases, many of which have no odour, making it extremely difficult (if not impossible) to get down the stairs and escape by the normal route. At best, there are only two to four minutes in which to survive being overcome by fumes. Deadly carbon monoxide is always present during fires, even though you cannot see or smell it. As though that were not enough, heat generated from foam furniture fires rapidly builds up to temperatures that can melt metal. Fire needs air for combustion, and foam contains pockets of air which act like little bunsen-burners, spreading the flames.

14

ACTION TO TAKE WITH FOAM FURNITURE FIRES

Your immediate natural reaction on seeing a foam furniture fire start would probably be to get some water. But it takes time, longer than you think, to get to the nearest tap, find something to put the water in, and then return with it to fight the fire—and time is the one thing you lack. A few breaths of poisonous fumes can knock you unconscious.

If a fire involving foam does start—do not try to tackle it yourself, get everyone out of the room where the fire is, then close the door in order to confine the spread of flames, smoke and fumes. See that everyone gets out of the house, then call the fire brigade.

AVOIDING FOAM FURNITURE FIRES

Fires do not always need flames to make them start, as heat often comes before flames. When combustible material gets hot enough, for example when placed near to an electric fire, the radiant heat will cause it to burst into flames on its own. This happens frequently and, in one instance, two children pushed an armchair too close to the electric fire in the sitting-room, and spontaneous combustion led to flames. Their mother was in the adjoining kitchen but knew nothing of the fire. When she opened the door and went into the room, both children were dead—overcome by lethal smoke-gases.

Gas fires, open fires and other sources of heat can produce the same result, but despite these and numerous other tragedies, foam furniture continues to sell world-wide. If we question this, we are reminded that the material cannot burst into flames on its own. That can only happen through misuse or carelessness on our part. However, regulations to protect the consumer and make upholstered furniture more fire-resistant are already in operation in some countries, and other countries have regulations on the way.

Not everyone can afford the old-fashioned horse-hair fillings, which have a much slower rate of fire development and thus give more time to escape to safety. Or kapok, or the newer padding materials which may eventually replace polyurethane foams, or the upholstery sprays and special treatments which can make furniture flame-retardant or resistant. So those with polyurethane, or latex, foam furniture fillings must be warned to take great care when lighting matches or smoking, and must take care to keep furnishings away from sources of heat.

HOW FIRES START

Fires do not start on their own. They start as a result of neglect or lack of care and thought on our part, usually in the way we least expect. The recipe for fire requires three things—material which will burn, heat and air. Without all three there cannot be fire. Remove any one of them and the fire will go out.

Take a typical Sunday (although it could equally well happen on any other day). You finish reading the newspaper and put it down on the coffee table or the floor or maybe a chair. You leave the room for any one of a dozen reasons and as you intend to return again shortly, you leave the electric fire on. It has a fixed guard fitted to the appliance, so you imagine it should be safe. While you are out, a gust of wind comes in through a door or window, blows the paper towards the fire and it finishes up resting against the guard. Within seconds the paper is alight and so is the carpet—and unless someone arrives promptly to do something about it, so is the sitting-room, and maybe your house.

Maybe you avoid leaving loose papers around unless they are weighted down with something—but what about that mirror on the sitting-room wall? That might cause a fire. How? By setting you alight.

Many mirrors are placed on walls above open fireplaces or radiant heaters. This forces people to get close and lean forward to use them, with the risk that their clothing will catch fire.

Do not place letters, invitations or Christmas cards on the mantelpiece, though nearly everyone does this. Think about the hazard.

Everyone knows a magnifying glass can be used to focus the sun's rays onto paper to set it alight. Most of us probably did this as children. But what about the magnifying glasses and spectacles which are left around our homes? These too can focus the scorching rays of the sun as it comes in through the windows. How many fires have been caused by this? So put such things safely away in a case or drawer.

TELEVISION FIRES

Most homes have television and this can be another less obvious cause of fire. We are told to switch the television off when not in use, at the set and at the socket, and remove the plug from the wall socket before we go to bed. If we do not do *all* these things, there could be a fire. What we are not told, and what is not appreciated, is that a black and white television generates at least 10,000 volts—and a colour television more than 20,000 volts. These voltages stay for quite a while after the set has been turned off. No domestic electric cable or house wiring is capable of carrying this voltage—and wires, plugs and sockets overheat if overloaded and could start a fire.

Television sets are often placed in built-in bookcases or on enclosed shelves—this is dangerous. Sets need circulating air for ventilation and cooling and if they are denied it they may overheat and catch fire. The

The high voltages generated by a television set can cause a 'delayed-action' fire. When not in use, television sets must be switched off at the set *and* at the socket. Remember—remove the plug from the wall socket before you go to bed.

holes in the casing at the back are for ventilation, so sets should be kept clear of the wall, curtains and soft furnishings.

If ever a peculiar smell is detected coming from a television set, it should serve as a warning and never be ignored. Something is wrong and a fire could start, after you have left the room, or even a few days later, unless a television engineer is called in immediately to check things and put them right. Because of the high voltages involved—never touch the back or inside of the set yourself *even when it is unplugged.*

KEEPING ELECTRICITY UNDER CONTROL

When fires are shown on television or reported in the newspapers, it is invariably stated that the cause is believed to have been an electrical fault. Subsequent investigations and research show that a high proportion of all fires are, in fact, attributed to electrical causes, but the phrase 'due to an electrical fault' can be misleading. Electricity is perfectly safe if used properly, and 'faults' only occur through deterioration and neglect, or the misuse of electric appliances and installations on our part. We cannot blame electricity—only ourselves.

Homes can be made a great deal safer, lives can be saved, and serious injuries reduced through care and commonsense in keeping electricity under control. If we fail to do this, we could easily receive an electric shock or start a fire. As the causes and prevention of both these hazards are closely interlinked and dependent on the other—fuller coverage is given in the chapter on *Electrical Safety*. The general points which now follow should help ensure that electricity does not cause a fire in the home.

MAINS AND PLUG FUSES

One of the first things to know is where the electricity mains is situated in your home, so that you can turn it off without delay in an emergency. The electrical circuits in your home are protected by mains fuses on the consumer unit, or on a separate panel close to the mains switch. There should also be fuses in the plugs to each appliance. The purpose of the fuses is to serve as a weak link in the installation, and to act as a safety device to interrupt the current, 'blow', when there is overloading or other fault in the circuit or appliance. The older type of fuseboard contains rewirable fuses, while modern ones have cartridge fuses.

If a mains fuse blows always *turn off the main switch* before attempting to replace the fuse. You will need a torch if it is night or the cupboard is dark, and it always pays to have spare fuse-wire or cartridges handy. With the rewirable type of fuses, look for scorch marks or wire breaks when locating the faulty fuse. Always use fuse-wire of the correct size, this will be marked on the fuse carrier. Cartridge fuses are easier to replace—but it is less easy to detect scorch marks or know which cartridge has blown, as the fuse-wire is hidden inside the sealed cartridge. One way of checking which cartridge has blown, is to remove the base of a metal-cased torch and place one end of the fuse on the bottom of the battery and the other end on the torch casing. If the bulb fails to light when the torch is switched on it means the fuse has blown. Always replace the fuse with one of the correct rating for the job. Never use a thicker wire in a rewirable fuse or a larger cartridge in a cartridge fuse, even as a temporary measure, and never attempt to replace cartridge fuses with wire.

Some installations have *miniature circuit breakers* (M.C.B.). Once the fault has been fixed, you simply press the button, or click on the switch, to restore power.

Plugs throughout the house, garage, sheds and workshops should be correctly wired. They should also contain the right fuse, as electrical appliances operate at different wattages (which are marked on them, usually at the back or base), with higher wattages requiring 13 amp fuses and lower wattages requiring 3 amp fuses.

Normally, 3 amp fuses are used up to 700 watts, and 13 amp fuses from 700 to 3,000 watts. There are exceptions—some colour televisions and some appliances, such as vacuum cleaners and spin dryers—which, though rated at less than 700 watts, require a high starting current and thus require a 13 amp fuse. The manufacturer's instructions for each appliance will tell you which fuse to use in the plug, but if there is any doubt, seek advice from the electricity authority or from a fully qualified electrician.

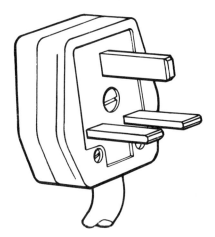

70 million out of 400 million electric plugs in use in Britain's homes could be faulty and could prove lethal. Always purchase plugs of a reliable make and if in doubt seek expert advice.

Remember, the fuses at the mains and in the plugs are there for our protection. If fuses keep blowing we should not keep replacing them. They are a warning of potential fire. Get a qualified electrician to find the cause and correct it.

Fuller details on mains and appliances, plugs and fuses, and the correct wiring of plugs, together with many more tips, are included in the chapter on *Electrical Safety*.

Care is needed when buying plugs. They tend to look alike but it does not pay to buy the cheapest. See that they conform to the necessary safety standards, as sub-standard plugs may have loose pins which fail to fit tightly into the socket; arcing can then occur, with consequent over-heating and further danger of fire.

We are warned, frequently, never to pull plugs out of sockets by the flex. If we ignore this advice, the wires inside can work loose, touch, fail to earth appliances and start a fire.

Many homes have insufficient socket outlets, and adaptors which turn a single outlet into a multiple one are popular and readily available. They need to be used with caution, as there is a grave danger of overheating, which is a major source of fires in the home. The wires become white hot, burning off their protective insulation and sending out sparks, often behind skirting boards or under floors. The ideal is, *one appliance, one socket*, certainly not three or more.

Flexes can be another potential hazard. They should be checked regularly and treated with care. If there are signs of fraying or wear, they should be replaced. Running flexes under carpets or linoleum is asking for trouble as walking over them wears the protective insulation away.

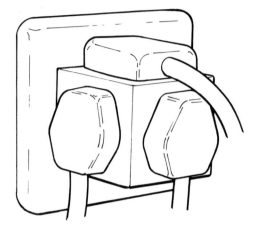

Overloaded adaptors are dangerous and are a major cause of fire. No more than two extra outlets per socket should be used. Certainly not three or more.

If the wires touch, there is a short circuit and someone could get a shock. There might even be a fire, at night, possibly, when everyone has gone to bed.

Never extend flexes with insulating tape, use proper connectors. The safest thing to do if a flex is not long enough is to get a new one.

On a more general note, always switch off and remove the plug of an electric appliance when not in use—and make sure you have all appliances serviced regularly. Switch off irons (even when fitted with thermostats), kettles, and the heat under pans if you are called to answer the door bell or telephone, or if you have to leave the room for any reason. Your attention may be distracted, or what you went to do may take longer than you imagined.

Keep electric fires and heaters well away from beds, furniture and furnishings, and never drape clothing or anything over storage radiators. Take special care with time-switched heaters and make sure they are well clear of curtains and furnishings at all times.

Time-switches and delay controls must never be fitted to radiant heaters. Every radiant fire should have a permanent safety guard. Where there are children, an adequate fireguard *must* also be fixed in front of it.

Do not dim lamps or lights by covering them, buy a low-wattage bulb, or one of the approved permanent wall-type dimmer switches.

Fires can be caused by using too powerful a bulb for a particular type of shade. The higher the wattage the greater the heat given off by the lamp. So check when buying a lampshade which wattage of bulb should be used.

Dangers often lie in unexpected places. If clothes or other household items containing foam rubber are put into driers, they can heat to the ignition point of the foam and start a fire, and can continue to smoulder even when removed from the drier. For the same reason foam rubber should not be used to insulate the hot-water tank in your airing-cupboard. Use only approved fire-resistant insulation materials.

The airing-cupboard can have another hazard if it contains an immersion heater. Properly installed heat-resistant cable *must* be used but, in many cases, the electric flex still curves down from the top of the immersion heater and rests on a bare section of the hot tank (between the gaps when some types of insulating jackets are fitted). Or else it rests on the hot water pipes as the cable reaches across to the supply coming in from the wall. A check of several installations has shown cables to be damaged, with heat marks or even scorching. The safest course with all these cables, whether heat-resistant or not, is to secure them safely, so they cannot touch any part of the hot tank or water pipes. Remember, if a fire does result, the items of clothing and linen will fuel the fire and make it particularly hazardous.

If the flex in your airing-cupboard is too long, as most are, tie the cable to the wooden-slatted shelving, so that it is unable to touch any of the hot metal areas mentioned. This will also ensure that the cable does not get tugged when laundry or clothing is put in or taken out.

ELECTRIC BLANKETS

Electric blankets are still the main cause of many fires, although this can

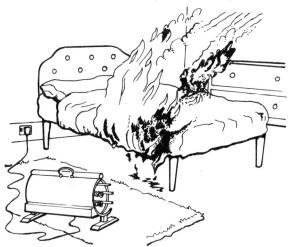

Keep all heaters well away from bedding, curtains and furniture.

be avoided if the safety rules are followed. For a start, electric blankets should always be used according to the maker's instructions. Read these carefully before and after purchase and make sure you buy an officially approved type. Having bought one, be sure to have it serviced regularly by the manufacturers.

Never use an electric underblanket over you—or an overblanket under you.

Underblankets must lie flat and be securely tied to the mattress. Preheating underblankets must be switched off before you get into bed and must never be switched on again while the bed is occupied. The only exceptions are *all-night* underblankets which are rather more expensive and operate on a low voltage for maximum safety. Always be sure which type of blanket you have, particularly if it was given as a present, and make sure you use it correctly and wisely.

There are some overblankets which have special devices to permit all-night use in complete safety. Overblankets should be used over the top sheet with just a light covering on top.

Water and electricity are lethal partners. Never switch a blanket on if it is wet, and do not switch it on to help it dry out either. Let it dry naturally. Always keep your electric blanket dry and flat—and never use a hot-water bottle as well as an electric blanket. They must be kept flat, as folds and creases can cause overheating.

USING GAS SAFELY

As with electricity, it is important to know where to turn off the main gas supply. It is also important to read the more general, and fuller, information given in the chapter on *Gas Safety*.

Regular servicing of all appliances by a qualified engineer or fitter is essential. This should include flexible tubing. Gas water-heaters, and central heating boilers and systems should be checked annually, with attention being given to flues and ventilators, to make sure they do not become blocked or obstructed. As with any heat source, gas fires and heaters should be kept well away from furnishings.

If the gas supply is interrupted, or you have a coin meter and the gas runs out, make sure you turn off all taps and appliances, and that they remain off, until you are ready to relight them. Remember to relight the pilot lights.

IF YOU SMELL GAS

If you smell gas you should:

(*a*) Put out cigarettes and do not use matches or naked flames.

(*b*) Do not operate electrical switches—neither on nor off. If there is a gas leak this could cause an explosion and fire.

(*c*) Open doors and windows to get rid of the gas.

(*d*) Check to see if a tap has been left on accidentally, or if a pilot light has gone out.

(*e*) If not, there is probably a gas leak. So turn off the whole supply at the meter and call the emergency gas service.

(*f*) If you cannot turn off the supply, or the smell continues after you have, call the emergency gas service immediately or ask someone else to do so.

If a tap has not been left on accidentally and the smell goes after you have turned off the supply, there is probably a gas leak from the pipes in your premises. This must be repaired by a competent person, and you must not turn the gas on again until the repair has been completed.

LIQUID PETROLEUM GAS

Liquid petroleum gas (L.P.G.) in the form of Butane or Propane is used widely in the home—either permanently for cooking, heating and lighting or as a stand-by in the event of a power cut. The difference between these gases and mains gas is that they can be stored as a liquid, taking up about $\frac{1}{200}$ th of the space needed to store it as a gas. The liquid turns to gas very easily, and gas fills the space above the liquid in the cylinder. As gas is drawn off in use, more liquid turns to gas to replace it.

The cylinders should be treated with care and should never be stored or carried upside-down. They must always be used in an upright position, otherwise the liquid could get into the supply lines and this would have serious results. The cylinders should never be subjected to heat, because the pressure inside might build up to a point beyond the designed safety limit, and an explosion could be caused. Both gases are heavier than air, so, if there is a leak, the gas will collect at a low level and will become dangerous in the presence of flame or a spark. For this reason cylinders should never be stored or used in cellars or below ground level.

As Propane is contained under higher pressure than Butane, Propane cylinders should be kept outdoors away from sun light and should never be stored or used indoors. Permanent installations should be fitted and piped into the home to appliances by an approved specialist. To make identification easy, Propane is stored in **red** cylinders, and Butane in **blue** or **green** cylinders.

Never change cylinders in the presence of naked lights, and do not move heaters while lit.

If a leak is suspected, never use a naked light to trace it. Turn the gas off, open all doors and windows, and make sure you have not overlooked any source of ignition. Examine all the pipes and connections. If the source of the leak is not evident, brush over the connections with a liquid detergent. This will bubble where there is a leak.

Maintenance is important as appliances need regular servicing and cleaning by qualified persons to keep them safe and operating efficiently and economically.

OIL HEATERS

These should be of a reputable make and fixed to the wall or floor so they cannot get knocked over by children or pets. They should also be kept level and out of draughts. It does not pay to buy old paraffin heaters as they may lack the safety features of modern types.

Oil heaters should be refilled out of doors, and never whilst still burning, with care being taken not to overfill them. The fuel must be kept in a safe, cool place and the appliance must be kept clean and regularly serviced by a dealer.

The heaters must never be moved while alight, and the standard advice about not putting clothing or other fabrics on top of appliances applies as it does with *all* other heaters. If tempted to break this rule, remember the death of a two-year-old boy who had a slight cold, so his mother moved a paraffin heater into his bedroom. By the time the fire was discovered, the little boy was dead. Suffocated by smoke and fumes from a blanket he had thrown from his cot onto the heater.

OPEN FIRES

Chimney fires are still common, with a large proportion of them spreading to the rest of the house and even to adjacent property. If the wall gets hot or if the chimney catches fire, call the fire brigade. You can avoid these hazards by having your chimneys swept regularly. Soot burns readily, so, if you use non-smokeless fuel, including wood, your chimney should be swept at least twice a year. If you use smokeless fuel your chimneys should be swept once a year. Be sure the hearth and surround are kept clean.

An effective sparkguard, with a fine mesh, fixed in front of a fire, is essential in rooms used by children or elderly people, and the last adult to leave a room where a fire is burning must see that a sparkguard is in place. It should be a fully enclosed guard, covering the top as well

A secure fine-mesh sparkguard fixed in front of a fire is essential for the protection of children and elderly people. Sparkguards should be used in rooms that are left empty.

as the sides and front, and should be able to clamp to the fireplace sur-round or wall.

Do not bank the fire too high, apart from the risk of a chimney fire, burning coal or wood could fall onto the floor. Never carry hot coals from one fire to light a fire in another room and never use petrol or paraf-fin to light a fire or revive it. Do not use newspaper to make it draw; use a draught tin or a metal tray. Ashes must never be put in cardboard or wooden boxes, use a metal ash-can, preferably a covered one.

Do not dry clothes by, or place armchairs too close to, an open fire, even if it has a guard in front of it. Make sure all fires are safe before the family retires to bed.

THE MOST DANGEROUS ROOM
The kitchen is the most dangerous room in the house, with the living-room coming a close second, which is not really surprising as these are the two rooms where the most activity takes place.

Many cupboards and shelves contain highly flammable and explosive liquids, such as turpentine or turpentine substitute, methylated spirit, dry cleaning fluid, paint, paint strippers, solvents, polishes, varnishes, lac-quers, adhesives and insecticides. These should only be kept in the house in small amounts (and out of reach of children), in clearly labelled containers, with stoppers, away from all sources of heat.

Read any warnings and instructions before you use dangerous liquids and make sure you have extinguished all naked flames. Turn off all gas and electrical appliances—and do not smoke. Always try to select polishes, paint strippers and other products which have a non-flammable base.

If you have no outside shed or garage, then no more than two gallons of any flammable liquid, less if possible, should be stored in the house, in a cool place.

Petrol must not be used in the house, to clean clothes or for any other purpose, as the vapours are highly flammable and extremely dangerous. In Britain it is illegal to store petrol inside a house. You can store up to four gallons in the garage, in two-gallon containers, but they must be metal containers and properly labelled. Even in the garage, extreme care is needed.

Safety precautions in the kitchen, to avoid fire hazards, include never leaving teacloths or washing over the cooker to dry. See that flexes from electric kettles and other appliances are never allowed to rest on, or drag over, the cooker, and see that the clothes you and others are wearing never come into contact with cooker rings.

Whenever possible, it is best to keep children out of the kitchen; certainly never leave them there unattended. When cooking, always make a point of turning handles inwards, while making sure that the handles are never positioned over a heat source, whether electricity or burning gas. A simple guard can be purchased for fixing to a cooker to prevent handles and pans being tipped over by children or adults.

The handles of pans on a cooker should always be turned away from the reach of children.

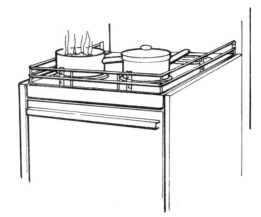

Safety guards make cooking safer still and protect children from boiling pans.

Spilt oil or fat, whether on the cooker, working surfaces or the floor, should always be wiped clean immediately, to prevent the risk of fire or falls.

HOW TO AVOID CHIP-PAN FIRES

Fires involving fats or oils are alarming because they happen so suddenly, with flames gathering power and reaching threateningly towards the ceiling. One of the most frequent causes of a chip-pan fire is being called away to answer the frontdoor or telephone. The only way to avoid this is to remove the pan from the heat before leaving the kitchen. An unattended pan must *never* be left on the heat.

Chip-pan fires are more frequent than you might imagine, but they can be avoided. Pans should never be more than one-third full of oil or fat, nor filled with too much food at a time. Never heat oil to a blue haze; if the oil or fat starts to smoke, then it is overheating and about to ignite.

Never put a lid on a deep-fat pan when heating or frying, as this might lead to condensation dripping into the hot fat and cause a fire. Tight fitting lids are not recommended on chip-pans unless they have safety valves or cut-out apertures.

HOW TO PUT OUT A CHIP-PAN FIRE

When a chip-pan catches fire, one's instinct is to pick it up and remove it from the heat source, or take it to the sink, or, worst of all, take it out of doors. These things must never be done. The first thing to do is turn off the heat and cover the pan with a lid, a large plate or a wet tea towel. If using a tea towel, wet it under a tap and wring it out quickly,

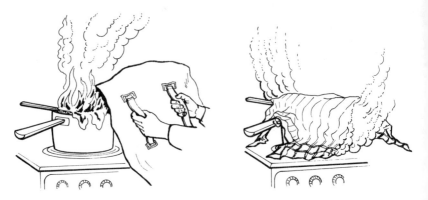

Never move a chip-pan which has caught fire and never attempt to douse the flames with water. Turn off the heat source and extinguish the flames by smothering them with a lid, an approved fire blanket or a wet *but wrung out* tea towel—held at an angle of 45° to the pan and sloping upwards in front of you to protect you from the flames. Let the pan cool before removing the covering, otherwise the oil or fat could re-ignite.

until just damp, then use it to smother the fire. On no account put a dripping or very wet cloth over the pan, or try to use water (or sand) to put out the fire. Burning fat will cascade all over you and all over the kitchen.

An alternative to the tea towel method of smothering fire is to use one of the approved fire blankets available. But whatever is used, whether a lid, damp tea towel or fire blanket, it should be held at an angle of about 45° to the chip-pan, sloping upwards in front of you to protect you from the flames. If you do not do this, and you place the smothering object flat down on to the pan, the flames are likely to fan out and burn you severely.

If you have been successful in smothering the fire, do not remove the covering as there is always a possibility that the oil or fat will re-ignite. Leave the pan and its cover for half-an-hour or until it has completely cooled down.

AEROSOLS

Aerosols are so convenient and so easy to operate that there are few homes that do not have an aerosol of some sort in them. There are more than 200 different aerosols on sale in Great Britain alone. From air fresheners to hair sprays and from shaving creams to all manner of household cleaners and medicinal sprays.

These are perfectly safe, provided the simple instructions, printed on the containers, are followed. Like many articles, misuse can be hazardous, and we must remember that the contents are under pressure. When aerosols are heated, their contents expand and their internal pressure increases, thus, at some stage, the aerosol must burst. All aerosols must be kept away from sources of heat. This includes ledges over radiators and places where rays of sunlight can reach them, particularly when penetrating through glass.

The contents and uses of aerosols are so varied that it is important to read the safety instructions for *each* aerosol you buy. Having read the instructions on one aerosol many people imagine they apply to all aerosols, but things are not that simple. Some are flammable, others non-flammable. The safest practice is to read every label, and never use aerosols near naked flames or any incandescent material; never use aerosols when you are smoking and never pierce or burn the containers, even when empty. Store aerosols in a safe place, out of the reach of children at all times, and do not burn them when empty, put them in the dustbin.

Sometimes there are additional instructions to enable you to get the best use from your aerosol. Make a point of reading the printed instructions on each container, as new products and fresh applications are being developed all the time.

CARELESS SMOKING

Each year thousands of fires and many deaths are caused by matches and careless smoking. Both have tremendous kindling power, with temperatures approaching the heat given out by the elements of a 1,000 watt electric fire.

Great danger is caused by people dozing off while smoking in an armchair or in bed. *Never do this.* The chances are you will be suffocated, and die without the fire waking you, by smouldering furnishings or bedding. A survey taken in the U.S.A. showed that around 70% of all cigarette fire fatalities were due to smokers dozing off.

Homes should always contain plenty of ashtrays. Even if you do not smoke, your visitors might. Ashtrays should be deep, and cigarettes, cigars, pipes and matches should be extinguished completely, not left to continue burning. All cigarettes must be stubbed out before you go to bed.

Saucers or plates are not suitable as ashtrays, as cigarettes can roll off. Use proper ashtrays, placed on a firm object such as a table—never put them on the settee. Do not place a partly smoked cigarette or cigar on an ashtray, intending to resume smoking a few seconds later. Cigarettes can fall off ashtrays, and those seconds tend to become minutes, and if you leave the room there is always the chance you will forget all about your still-burning cigarette.

Be careful when emptying ashtrays. Cigars and cigarettes can take a considerable amount of extinguishing and, if anyone has been smoking recently, the cigar or cigarette might still be alight without you realising it. Thus it is dangerous to empty ashtrays, or throw matches into waste-paper baskets (even metal ones) or kitchen waste and pedal bins.

Children are fascinated by matches and lighters, and they start thousands of fires innocently or out of curiosity. These objects should be kept out of their reach and out of their sight.

Keep lighter fuel containers away from heat and do not smoke or stand near naked flames or heating appliances when refuelling a lighter.

CANDLES

It is a tragedy, but also a fact of life, that unsafe goods come onto the market. Some of the candles intended for cake decoration are one example. They were available through mail order, as well as in some shops, before the warnings went out—and retailers stopped stocking and selling them. There was no problem while the candles were on the cake. The trouble arose when people took the candles off the cake and tried to dispose of them, having blown them out. Although extinguished, they kept relighting of their own accord. Time and again each candle was extinguished and relit itself shortly afterwards. As Christmas was approaching there was the added danger that people might put them on Christmas trees, and warnings were issued from the fire services, explaining that the only way the candles could be put out safely was to totally immerse them in water for a considerable period and then to dispose of the remains by burying them.

This shows how careful we need to be when purchasing anything, and how important it is to go for proven products.

Whenever there is a power cut, out come the candles. As candles are not used very often, people are inclined to be careless with them. Remember to keep the candles upright, firmly in holders, on a level surface well away from curtains and furnishings, and away from draughts. Make sure you extinguish them completely when you have finished with them.

Candles should never be used in children's bedrooms to serve as night-lights. Use a proper low-wattage mains or battery night-light.

Never put candles on a Christmas tree. Use fairy lights and always check that they are in good working order before switching on the electricity supply. Beware of the additional fire hazards presented by decorations, wrapping paper, cards, paper hats and crackers, and candles, if these are used on the dining table. This rule also applies to birthdays and any other days when decorations might be used.

ATTICS

Naked flames, such as candles and matches, should never be taken into the attic, and never smoke there either. If light is required, use a lead-lamp with a protected guard, or a torch. Fires, or blowlamps, must not be used to unfreeze pipes. Have the pipes lagged and you will be safe, avoid freeze-ups and save on fuel costs.

UNDERSTAIRS CUPBOARDS

Most households regard the cupboard under the stairs as the place to store things out of sight. What we must *not* store there, however, are flammable liquids and materials, newspapers or rubbish. If a fire starts there, or elsewhere, the hall and stairs can act as a chimney spreading the fire rapidly and increasing its intensity with terrifying results.

SAFEGUARDING CHILDREN

Every year in Britain around 200 children die in fires, with many thousands more dying throughout the world and countless others suffering serious burns. Many of the ways of safeguarding children have already been covered, but there are still other important points that must be mentioned.

Children should never be left alone in a house. Even if they behave themselves, there are always things beyond their control, things that can go wrong and start a fire. If you have to leave your children, get a reliable friend, relation or neighbour to look after the children and keep them safe. An adult should know what to do in the event of fire.

If nursery windows or children's bedroom windows are guarded with bars, then make sure the bars are removable in the event of fire. In certain circumstances, a window may be the only means of escape or rescue.

FIREWORKS

It is interesting to note that since a firework safety code was introduced in Great Britain over ten years ago, and was given wide and continuous publicity, accidents involving injury have been halved, but that still leaves over a 1,000 accidents a year. Which shows that while it pays to have dangers pointed out, there is still a way to go. Apart from personal injury, there is always the risk of starting fires.

Fireworks should be used out of doors, and should always be treated with respect. Water, sand and a first aid kit must be kept close at hand. The fireworks should be kept in a secure container—wood or tin—with the lid being replaced after the selection of a firework. Fireworks should not be handled by young children. You will need a torch to read the instructions on each firework; having read the instructions, follow them.

Never try to read the instructions by the light of a bonfire or naked flames, and never smoke when handling fireworks.

Make sure all aerial fireworks, such as rockets, are angled away from spectators, also check that they are angled away from your house and other property, so that the falling sticks and empty cases do not cause damage. Light the end of the firework fuse at arm's length, preferably with a safety firework lighter or fuse wick. Stand well back, and never allow anyone to return to a firework once lit—it may explode in their face. Any dud fireworks should be left for at least half an hour and, even then, treat them with care. Watch out for a sudden change of wind that could cause sparks or send your fireworks in the wrong direction.

If you are giving a firework party explain the safety rules to everyone first, adults and children, especially children, and keep them well organised. Make sure that no one throws fireworks, or puts a firework in their pocket. If you decide to have a bonfire, be extra careful, and

This is wrong! Site bonfires carefully, allowing for changes in wind direction. Always keep an eye on bonfires and stand upwind from them. A few breaths of the fumes from certain rubbish can kill.

Always fill lawnmowers out of doors, never in a garage or shed. Check that the machine is switched off and the spark plug disconnected. Petrol can produce a vapour trail of 50 metres (55 yards)—and a small spark can cause a catastrophe.

keep it well away from the fireworks, fences, hedges, trees and long grass. Do not use petrol or paraffin to light it, and do not burn dangerous rubbish such as flammable liquids, paints or aerosols.

When the firework display is over, make sure the bonfire has been put out. If all the safety rules are followed, accidental injury and fires will be avoided and everyone can enjoy themselves. But do have a thought for pets and keep them safely indoors—the sound and sight of fireworks is anything but fun for them.

THE GARDEN, GARAGE AND SHEDS
Firework evenings are not the only times people light bonfires. Whatever the kind of bonfire, the same safety precautions apply about not using petrol or paraffin to get them going or keep them going, and about keeping them away from the house, wooden fences, sheds, trees and bushes. Unattended bonfires can be extremely dangerous, so keep an eye on them. Avoid sparks and watch out for changes in wind speed and direction, which can result in bonfires getting out of control and setting fire to

neighbouring property, thatched roofs, copses and woods. Allow for this possibility when you site your bonfire.

Outside the home may seem safer than inside where fire is concerned, but the risks of fire are still considerable, and they often arise from a combination of circumstances. Someone may need to mow the lawn with a motor-mower, so they fill the petrol tank, correctly leaving the motor switched off, but they fill it inside the garage. That could cause a fire. Petrol can produce a 50 m (55 yd) vapour trail, and a small spark can cause a catastrophe. The only safe place to fill a petrol tank, whether it belongs to a car, motor-cycle or motor-mower, is out of doors where the concentration of petrol vapour is rapidly dispersed.

Do-it-yourself enthusiasts, and those who only do the odd job, should never smoke in garages or workshops. Shavings should be cleared up after carpentry. Always use non-flammable do-it-yourself materials whenever possible. Use properly installed, earthed 3 pin sockets for electric tools, never run them from a lamp socket. Some electric tools are 'all insulated' or 'double insulated' for maximum safety. If greater illumination is needed, naked lights should never be used, use a protected lead-

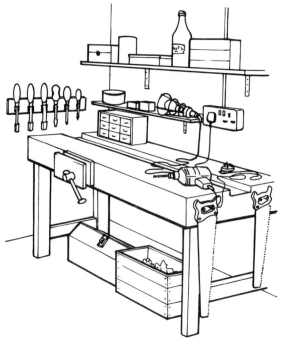

Tidy workshop with wood-shavings cleared away, tools placed sensibly and everything ship-shape. Note the properly installed sockets for portable electric tools and the protected lead-lamp. These all help to ensure DIY safety.

lamp. As for blowlamps, even professionals frequently set fire to buildings, or start a small fire which smoulders and then bursts into flame after they have left the site. So be careful when using a lighted blowlamp, and never leave it unattended.

Not everyone appreciates the possible hazard caused by a build up of hydrogen when batteries are being charged. This should only be done where there is plenty of ventilation, away from naked lights. Make sure the battery-charging equipment is of an approved, safe, type.

FIRE WARNING SYSTEMS

Although fire brigades can get to the scene of a fire within three to four minutes in city areas, the further your home is from the nearest fire station, the longer it will take. No matter where you live, and you should certainly consider it if you live in a country area, you might want to install a smoke detector and automatic fire-alarm system.

The two main smoke detectors in general use are either of the *photo-electric* or *ionisation* type. The *photoelectric* type tends to be best at detecting slow, smouldering fires, while the *ionisation* models are best at detecting a sudden outbreak of fire. You may wish to install both types to cover both situations, a system of detectors and alarms will complete the protection of your home. New research and development may come up with other types and systems, and the best advice is to ask your local fire brigade for their opinion, in relation to your particular circumstances. Avoid door-to-door salesmen.

FIRE EXTINGUISHERS AND FIRE BLANKETS

Insuring your home and its contents is something you should do as a matter of course, but not everyone thinks of purchasing fire-fighting equipment. If you lose the contents of your home in a fire, insurance money will buy new goods, but it cannot replace your much loved possessions. The right kind of fire-fighting equipment could protect your goods and property, and it might even save lives. Once again, ask your local fire brigade for advice on the best equipment to buy. They will be pleased to help, because, if you are able to prevent a small fire from becoming a large one, you and everyone in your home will be safer and the firemen will be at less risk. They, like everyone else, want to live long enough to enjoy their pensions.

Heavy, old-fashioned fire extinguishers are becoming things of the past, modern fire extinguishers are comparatively light and simple to use. Some are water based and others deliver a concentration of carbon dioxide, and there are other kinds, but the choice, and use, depends on the type of fire. There are also certain, fully approved, all-purpose dry-powder fire extinguishers, which are non-conductors of electricity and which can be used for almost all types of fire in the home. However, they should not be used for oil and fat fires, as these should be dealt with by use of a fibreglass fire blanket.

LAST THING AT NIGHT
It was mentioned earlier that fire needs three things to exist, material which will burn, heat and air. It follows that a fire can be prevented from spreading, even forced to go out, if starved of air. So it is a wise precaution to close kitchen and living-room doors before you go to bed. Another precaution is to sleep with the bedroom door closed. Many fire deaths occur upstairs from fires started downstairs. A closed bedroom door will help keep fire at bay. Most first-floor fatalities were found with the bedroom door open, the victims being overcome by smoke and hot gases rising up the staircase.

Having closed all doors, remember that this cannot always prevent a serious hazard arising, so do not relax any of your general fire precaution safeguards, as these are designed to prevent a fire from breaking out in the first place.

PUTTING OUT SMALL FIRES
Water from the nearest tap is still one of the best ways of putting out most fires in the home, except for electrical fires, unless the current has first been turned off at the mains. If the fire involves an electrical appliance, it must be switched off and unplugged before water is used. If possible, switch off at the mains, as this is sometimes quicker and is much safer, as the fire can spread to the skirting on the wall, or anywhere else that contains the electrical wiring circuits of the home.

Some of the experts recommend using buckets of water to put out a small oil heater fire. But, if you do this, you must stand at least six feet (two metres) away from the fire, in case the fire flares up. Do not attempt to remove or carry the oil heater, and once you have dealt with the heater fire, tackle the surrounding fire. Extreme care is needed, water will put out an oil fire on a carpet, but if water spills onto linoleum, it is more likely to spread the burning paraffin. If the fire gets out of hand, get out of the room and shut the door behind you.

Water is ideal for putting out chimney fires and those involving wood or paper.

Having extinguished a fire, do not be over confident. Certain furnishings, such as the interior of a mattress, can smoulder for hours without you knowing, even after you have put out the flames and soused the mattress with water.

Everyone loves picturesque thatched cottages, but if you live in one, you must take great care inside—and outside, especially with bonfires. A spark from a passing tractor exhaust set the roof of a thatched house on fire, and a strong wind fanned the flames towards three detached but adjoining thatched houses and set them alight. One spark lit four thatched houses. It pays to have a tap readily available and a sufficiently long hose to reach any part of the thatch from the front, back or sides. A tap outside, or in a garage, will need to be lagged to prevent it from freezing up.

The way to deal with chip-pan fires has already been dealt with; foam furniture fires too, with a warning *not* to tackle it yourself, bearing in mind that the poisonous fumes can kill within a few breaths. Close the door, get everyone out of the house—and call the fire brigade.

IF CLOTHING CATCHES FIRE

If clothing catches fire, it is terrifying, and it is hardly surprising that people panic and rush about. However, this is the one thing they must not do, as it only fans the flames and makes things worse. If you are present when someone's clothing catches fire, immediately force them

If someone's clothing catches fire, force victim to the ground, grab the nearest suitable thing, blanket, rug, etc., and wrap it tightly round to smother the flames.

to the ground. Then grab a fire blanket and wrap it around them. If one is not available, use any heavy textile fabric, such as a rug, carpet, coat, overcoat, ordinary blanket, curtain, eiderdown, towel or dressing gown. Do not waste time searching, grab the first suitable thing close to hand.

If your clothing is on fire, drop to the floor and roll across the floor to extinguish the flames.

As you wrap it tightly round to smother the flames, be careful your own clothing does not catch fire.

If your own clothing is on fire, drop to the ground at once, to prevent the flames from travelling up to your face. Then roll across the ground to extinguish the flames.

CALLING THE FIRE BRIGADE

Fire fighting is a highly professional job, requiring training and continuous drills and practice. Amateurs should not attempt to do the job except in the case of small fires which can be tackled safely. If the fire cannot be extinguished immediately and safely, close the door to confine the spread of smoke and fire, and close the windows if you can reach them safely. Get everyone out of the house, then call the fire brigade, from a neighbour's house if you are unable to do so from your own.

In Britain, dial 999 and ask for **fire**. In some other countries, the fire brigade may have their own special number. Always keep this by the telephone, and try to remember it.

If you cannot see to dial 999, because of smoke or darkness, place two fingers in the two holes directly to the left of the finger stop. Remove the finger nearest stop. With the other finger now in '9' hole, rotate dial to finger stop. Release finger and allow dial to return. Repeat twice more. Those are the official instructions, and you can practise the routine without lifting the receiver or making a false call. Try with your eyes shut, so you are fully drilled should an emergency arise.

The next piece of advice can make the difference between life and death, between the fire being put out or your home being lost. When your 999 call is answered by the operator, and you are put through to

How to dial 999 when unable to see due to smoke or darkness. Do not lift the receiver when practising this or you will be making a false call. (See text for full instructions.)

fire, try to keep calm. Speak distinctly and give your address clearly. Give the number and/or the name of your house, your street and your town or village. **Do not hang up yet!** In the confusion, fire victims frequently just say their house is on fire, without saying which house and where. Or they give a wrong or incomplete address. This leaves fire engine crews unable to find your house unless they can see a fire burning, or someone else has reported it. In some cases people know they have a fire station down the road, and think they are talking to that station, instead of which, their call may have been put through to the area headquarters many miles away. Saying your home is on the opposite corner to the supermarket or the vicarage, and then slamming the telephone down, will only confuse the fire brigade, they have thousands of supermarkets or vicarages in their area, and you have not told them where you are, or which supermarket or vicarage you are talking about. So do not hang up, give your address properly and tell them whether anyone is still trapped in the building, and what type of fire it is. If you know someone requires an ambulance tell the fire brigade and they will call one for you. The fire brigade will repeat the information you have given them, to check that they have heard it correctly—and they may want to ask questions. This will not waste fire-fighting time, the fire crew for your area will already be alerted, and will be racing to man their vehicles while you are still talking. Remain on the telephone and do not put it down until the fire brigade have all the information they require. If you carry out this drill correctly, it will only take seconds.

If you forgot to tell them that an ambulance was needed, dial 999 and ask the telephone operator to put you through to **ambulance.**

It may be that you, or your neighbours, do not have a telephone. In which case go to the nearest call box and dial 999. You will not need

If you think a room is on fire do not investigate it until everyone has escaped from the building. Approach with caution. Stand well back against the wall and open the door slowly, with your face and body well away from the opening. If smoke sweeps out, close the door immediately. Call the fire brigade.

coins—it costs nothing—the operator will ask which emergency service you require, tell them **fire**.

ONCE OUT STAY OUT

One reason for fatalities and injuries in fires, is that people linger too long in the building. They stop to dress fully, or to rescue treasured possessions. At the first sign of smoke, get out of the building fast. *Walk don't run*, otherwise you might stumble, and not only injure yourself, but also injure others by causing a pile-up that blocks the exit for those behind you. Once everyone is out, they should stay out. Their lives are far more important than any material thing left inside.

If you live in a block of flats, use the emergency escape routes. The doors leading to them should always be kept shut, so close them after you have gone through.

People who live in bedsitters or in a house subdivided into flatlets should see that everyone else in the building is also alerted.

If you think a room is on fire, do not open the door to investigate until everyone has escaped from the building. Then approach the door with extreme caution. Feel it first with the back of your hand. If it is hot, *do not* open the door. The smoke and flames will blast out and engulf you with an explosive force that could hurl you across the hall or landing, or even down several flights of stairs. Even if the door is not hot, you must still be careful. Open it slowly, with your face well away from the opening. If smoke sweeps out, close the door immediately. Then get out of the building and wait for the fire brigade to arrive. They are equipped with breathing apparatus and can deal with the situation.

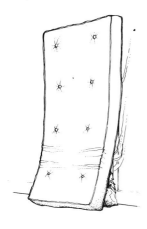

If you are trapped in a room by fire outside the room, and you cannot escape—shut the door and put a rug, blanket or towel at the bottom of the door. If possible put a mattress against the whole door, to keep out the deadly smoke. Then go to the window and shout for help.

WHAT TO DO IF TRAPPED BY FIRE

Stairs are often unusable by the time most fires have become established. If the fire is outside the room you are in, and you cannot escape that way, shut the door and put a rug, blanket or towel at the bottom of the door to keep out the poisonous smoke. Go to the window and shout for help, then wait for the fire brigade to arrive and rescue you.

If you are trapped in a room by fire, remember that heat and smoke rise, so get down low, where it will not only be cooler but where a supply of air will support life away from the poisonous fumes. Keep really low, within six inches (15 centimetres) of the floor.

The greatest dangers arise in the rooms upstairs. If the fire makes it impossible for you to remain in the room, you might, if you are young and athletic, be able to get out through the window. If you have to break a window, do not use your hands. Use a chair or similar hard object, or remove your shoe and break the glass with the heel. Do not attempt to kick it out with your shoes on, you could easily sever an artery in your leg. Protect your eyes and face with an improvised hood, a pillow or a solid object such as a wooden drawer.

Throw out any mattresses and pillows, if available, as these could break your fall, and be sure to relax as you land. Even a 15 foot (five metre) drop can kill or injure, and has done on many occasions. Alternatively, you can reduce the length of the fall by easing out, feet first, and hanging from the window-ledge, with your feet that much nearer the ground before letting go. If you can twist your body so that it is sideways on to the window and wall, so much the better. When you fall you will avoid falling backwards, which could end in severe injury to your legs, back,

Poisonous smoke is the real killer. This builds up in layers from the ceiling down, so keep low when making your escape. Remember, at six inches (15 cm) above the floor there is usually enough oxygen to support life.

neck or head, which might hit the lower window-ledge. Being sideways on, and pushing away slightly as you let go, will give you enough momentum to keep clear of the building, this will make your fall less hazardous. If you have thrown out something soft to land on, it will be useless unless you have thrown it where you propose to land.

For the not so young and the less athletic, jumping from a window is not to be recommended as it can be fatal. The answer, in this case, is to wait for rescue by the fire brigade. Continue to lean out of the window to get air, unless prevented from doing so by smoke or flame. In which case, lie close to the floor, where the air is safer and clearer, until you hear the fire brigade. If you have to shout, take a breath of air from ground level before standing up, then return to floor level to continue breathing the safer air.

For buildings with more than one upstairs floor, if you are above the first floor, *you should never attempt to jump*. In one terrible disaster, a tall multi-storey building caught fire in South America. The helicopters trying to rescue people from the upper floors had to abandon their attempt, as the upsurge of flames was so great. The fire brigade ladders could only reach a third of the way up the building, and people started to jump from the windows to certain death. Even when the firemen had tackled the fire, and the authorities shouted and pleaded with people not to jump, telling them that the fire was under control and that the fire brigade were already making their way up the staircases to the upper floors, the residents were so terrified they still continued to jump. Jumping from windows ten to 14 storeys high, they hoped to catch a ladder on the way down. Some jumped holding their possessions. Broken bodies littered the streets, and still they jumped. Yet one couple, an army officer and his wife did not panic and did all the right things. They survived while 119 other people perished trying to escape. Trapped on the twelfth floor, the couple stuffed wet towels around the cracks in the door and then placed a mattress against it to lessen the amount of dense smoke that was seeping through. They remained calm, and moved to a small bathroom window to breathe fresh air through its tiny opening. They did this for several hours. By doing the correct things, keeping calm and keeping their heads, they kept their lives and were finally rescued by firemen from one of the severest fires of all time.

SNATCH RESCUES
Earlier it was stated that once everyone was out of a burning building, they should stay out. Not returning to save treasures is one thing, but going back into the building to rescue children or adults is something quite different. One often sees a news item on television, or in the papers, where a house has caught fire with little apparent structural damage, there might be blackened brickwork around one window. We hear that a father or neighbour rescued everyone, except for a second or third child who died in the fire, but we are not told the correct procedure for rescuing trapped people. It can be important when time is short and it is too soon to expect the fire brigade to arrive. This vital problem is brushed aside, but it happens all too frequently, and we need to know what we can and should do to save lives.

Having raised this issue, it must be stated that **to return to a burning building is fraught with danger and often fatal.** It also makes things worse for the fire brigade when they do arrive, as they might have to rescue two people instead of one. Yet what parent can stand by without attempting to go back to rescue a child? If anyone is determined to go into the building under these circumstances, it is best that they know what they should, and should not, do. This will give their attempt a greater chance of success; remember that blindly dashing in invariably leads to death, not only for the rescuer but also for the person they were trying to rescue.

It takes courage to go into a burning building to carry out a 'snatch rescue'. Even fully trained firemen take a while to get used to it, and they have breathing apparatus, you do not.

Anyone who is hysterical should not attempt a snatch rescue, but an adult, in the right frame of mind, might be successful. The secret is to know what to do, and do it calmly.

If everyone is outside, and you want to rescue a child in an upstairs room, the answer is to keep low while going up the stairs. Keep your nose close to the ground, where the oxygen will be, and do not stand up. This is the whole secret, to keep down low, so that the heat and smoke go over your head. Smoke builds up in layers from the ceiling down, and smoke, as has been mentioned, is the real killer; but, even on an upper floor, there is an air current, six inches (15 centimetres) above the floor. This current will support life. If you stand up, you will never make it. The heat will knock you back and you will probably be killed by the fumes.

If you go up the stairs with your nose, literally, nearly touching the ground and if, when you get to the landing, you still do not stand up, you might make it to the bedroom and complete the rescue. Knowing that one must keep low, and remain low, is one reason why a fireman succeeds where a member of the public fails. If you rescue the child and keep the child at floor level, you can succeed. This is where courage comes in again, because your natural reaction is to stand up and run—**resist it.** You can make good progress, and so can the child or person being rescued, by going slowly and breathing the small amount of oxygen left at floor level.

Other things need to be taken into consideration if a snatch rescue is to be successful. The outer rails and edge of a staircase often get burnt or fall away, so keep to the wall side when going up and coming down. If smoke means that you cannot see, you must feel your way before proceeding, to make sure the stairs and floor are there. When you come to a closed door, whether of the bedroom or any other room, you may find it difficult to reach the door handle from your position close to the floor. *Do not* stand up in front of the door, if you do, quite apart from the dangers of poisonous smoke, you could be killed by a flash-over fire as air rushes in to replace the consumed oxygen, or you could be blasted off your feet.

Approach any door with extreme caution. You are faced with an extremely dangerous situation. Keep low by the wall at the side of the door, never in front of it, take a breath at low level, then reach up to the handle while holding your breath. (Remembering that you are now at the poisonous smoke level.) Kneel well back from the opening as you turn the handle, and drop your body flat to the ground. The door may well burst open, but you might be all right, as the main danger should pass above your head as you lie low to one side of the door.

Be careful, the handle could be hot. All this is difficult enough as it is, and if you damage your hand you will have difficulty in making the rescue. If you find it impossible to reach the handle from your crouched position by the wall, take a breath at low level, then stand up and, holding your breath and keeping the thickness of the wall between you and the room, keep well away from the door as you release the catch.

When things are as safe as they can be under such circumstances, crouch low as you enter the room and search for the child. Children tend to hide in awkward places, in wardrobes, under bedclothes, even under the bed. The child will be terrified, and you may have to be firm. Grab them and force them to the floor, and keep them at that level as the two of you make your escape out of the room and down the stairs. *Never stand up and run.* People die within a few paces of their own front door. Keep low and remain low until you are both safely out of the house.

The experts warn against being too ambitious. If you have to go further than the first floor, they advise against attempting a snatch rescue. Wait for the fire brigade, they will have breathing apparatus.

Another point to bear in mind is, if a fire has been burning for some time, there is always a danger that the smoke level might be right down to the floor.

If rescue is impossible by the stairway, the alternative is to use a ladder to reach a window. An army officer did this, when aroused from sleep in the small hours of the morning by a distraught mother whose two children were trapped on the upper storey of a house some yards away. The stairs were impassable and the only available ladder was too small, so he ran back to his house to get a larger one. Climbing the ladder, he took a deep breath before entering the bedroom window, grabbed the coughing eleven month child from her cot and handed her out of the window to a neighbour who had climbed the ladder. Then he took a deep breath out of the window and went back in, searching for the baby's three-year-old brother. Failing to find the boy, he returned to the window for air, then crouched low at floor level and searched the other bedrooms. The last room he reached looked as if it only had one bed, but a further search revealed another bed round the corner of what turned out to be an L-shaped room. It, too, looked empty. Then he saw a slight movement. The boy, huddled at the bottom of the bed under the bed-clothes, was grabbed and rescued.

Luckily, in this case, the smoke had not reached right down to the floor, and, being a man used to thinking and acting in a disciplined manner, he succeeded in rescuing the two children. He managed it without breathing apparatus and he made it because he did the right things. Many off-duty firemen have also succeeded when called upon to carry out snatch rescues without breathing apparatus. They succeed because they know what to do.

Many members of the ordinary public have failed attempting snatch rescues. If they had known what to do, they might have made it.

LIFE-SAVING FIRE DRILLS

The way to avoid fires is to prevent them from starting in the first place. However, if a fire does occur and it cannot be extinguished immediately and safely, it is vital to know the correct fire drill so that everyone in your home can escape to safety.

When people are asked what steps they would take in the event of a fire, many dismiss the question by saying 'great big ones'. But fire is not a joke. Work out how you and your family could escape from a fire in your home. It may seem easy but, more often than not, in the event it proves to be difficult. Plan the fire drill for your particular house or flat now, and get everyone to run through it until they know precisely what to do.

Fires have a habit of happening when you least expect them. They can be so frightening that they invariably arouse panic. Since most types of panic are caused by a fear of the unknown, if you know what you are faced with and what you should do, you can act accordingly in a safe and orderly way, without panic.

Start to plan safe escape routes now, they are important, even if you never have to use them. Remember, smoke contains gases which can kill quickly, so, even if you are able to keep away from the flames, you do not have much time to escape. Explain this to everyone and tell them not to waste time by dressing before leaving the building, and not to stop to collect belongings. Children often make no attempt to escape from burning buildings. They wait to be rescued, some hide in cupboards or under beds and some even rush into the bathroom and lock themselves in—warn them not to do this.

The upper rooms are the most dangerous places in the home because smoke and heat rise. Three out of every four victims die upstairs from fires that start downstairs. That is why it pays to close bedroom doors at night, to serve as an obstacle to fire. Close downstairs doors and windows before going to bed as this will help contain a fire. If there is a fire, always shut the doors (and windows, if you can do so safely) in the room in which the fire has broken out.

Plan escape routes for everyone, in every kind of situation, for every room, **now**! The nearest available exit is an obvious choice, and these, and landings and staircases must always be kept clear of obstruction. Make sure keys are handy for doors which are locked. If you have double-glazing, learn how to open this quickly, so that it does not hinder your escape in the event of fire.

Having planned and practised the fire drill and means of escape from every room, see that everyone reaches an agreed assembly point outside the building and see that they stay there. This means a quick check can be made that everyone is present, and that no one is trapped or lingering inside. Do not assemble just outside the building. Choose a point at the planning stage, some safe distance away from the building. It might be dark, so everyone must know exactly where to assemble. If you live in a block of flats, do not use a lift, fire might cause an electrical failure and you could be trapped. Use the approved fire exit doors and fire escapes. Having got everyone to safety your next step, in a real fire, would be to call the fire brigade.

People, especially children, tend to forget fire instructions, so practise your fire drill until everyone does it correctly. Try it again some months later, to check that they still remember what to do. Get them to run through the drill with their eyes closed, feeling their way, in case an electrical failure puts out the lights, or the smoke from a fire prevents them from seeing.

All this may seem reasonably straightforward, but escaping from a burning building is not easy. Once a fire has become established, the stairway frequently becomes impassable, so alternative escape routes must be planned. It may be that the only escape from an upstairs room is through a window, so it obviously pays to have a ladder, and to practise using it. The alternative to escaping through a window is to breathe fresh air through the window, or at floor level below the smoke, until the fire brigade arrives.

If every possible method of escape is practised in your family fire drills, everyone in your home could survive instead of becoming yet another unnecessary and tragic statistic!

3

WATCH YOUR STEP

FALLS—THE BIGGEST KILLER

It always comes as a shock to learn that falls account for almost half the accidents that occur in the home. They are the largest single cause of death or injury. Each year there are over 3,000 deaths and 500,000 injuries in England and Wales alone. The elderly make up the greatest number of such accidents, with more females, of all ages, being killed than males. The falls are not necessarily from a height, many accidents are caused by falls at the same level.

Everyone loses their balance at some time in their life, whether they are youthful, middle-aged or elderly, but the greatest risks of death or injury come at the two extremes, childhood and old age. When young people fall, because they are more agile and fitter, the falls are usually

Falls are the biggest killer in the home! These fatal accidents are not always from a height. They can be falls on the level. The text on How To Prevent Falls gives detailed advice on how to safeguard yourself and your family.

less serious. When an elderly person falls, they probably fracture a thigh bone. This, or some other injury, is followed by an enforced period of immobilisation—which may lead to pneumonia or other illness. This, in turn, often leads to death. Of those who survive, many never recover from their injuries and become confined to wheelchairs.

The laws of gravity are something we live with from the moment we take our first steps. When one thinks that this force holds the universe together, it is something of a miracle that we ever learn the skill needed to stand up, let alone move about. We all make mistakes, lose our balance, take a false step, trip or slip in and around the home. We can fall anywhere, downstairs, upstairs, off chairs, out of bed. We can fall in the bath, out of windows and off ladders. Children face the additional hazards of falling from prams, push-chairs, high-chairs and cots.

HOW TO PREVENT FALLS

A great deal of research has been carried out into how and why falls happen, and if we follow the advice of the experts, and act on the knowledge gained from the hospital casualty departments, there are ways in which we can make our homes safer and so avoid these accidents.

It may seem more dangerous to go steeplechasing, skiing, hang-gliding or parachuting than to remain at home, but if the number of accidents are related to the number of sportsmen who take part in these activities, home comes out as a far more dangerous place to be. Yet we still tend to make the stairs in our homes look like the Cresta Run, and we leave toys, books and other objects on the floor so it looks like a steeplechase course.

Starting with the staircase, the first essential is to see that these and the landing are adequately lit, with switches that can be operated both from the top and bottom. All stairs should have handrails, preferably on both sides. With uprights placed sufficiently close to each other to prevent children from falling through. If the uprights already fitted are too far apart, additional uprights or panels can easily remedy the situation. Do not forget to fix a safety gate or barrier at the top and bottom of the stairs. Approved makes can be purchased, if you do not want to make them yourself.

Another tip to help avoid falls on the stairs, is to lay carpets with the pile sloping upwards. Make sure all carpeting is securely fixed, and held with stair rods, if these are fitted. Frayed or worn carpets catch toes, and frequently cause falls. So do rugs or mats at the bottom of stairs. These should be anchored and never placed loose on polished surfaces. The treads of uncarpeted stairs should not be polished, leave the wood bare. It is a fallacy that rubber mats prevent slipping. In practice they do quite the reverse, and are the cause of many severe falls.

As soon as they are old enough, it is a good idea to teach children how to use the stairs safely, otherwise they will try it for themselves, and find out the dangers the hard and dangerous way. It is equally important that everyone learns to concentrate when going up or down the stairs. This calls for 100% concentration, and is not as easy as one might imagine, as the human brain is incapable of concentrating on two things at once. If we catch sight of a buff envelope from the tax man on the door mat, or the door bell rings and we are expecting someone, our concentration is broken and, whether depressed or happy, we are likely to trip or fall.

We should always keep one hand free for using the handrails, both hands if possible; then we can prevent falls, or save ourselves if we do misjudge things and start to fall. There are occasions when we need our hands to carry things upstairs or downstairs, this means ignoring the handrails. If we are neither young or old we can usually manage it, but

Well lit halls, stairs and landings with switches which can be operated from top and bottom, securely fixed carpeting and handrails on *both* sides of the stairs, all of these help prevent falls.

it never pays to be too ambitious. Never carry too much at once, and, whenever possible, use one hand for the rail and one hand for carrying. That way a minor fall can be prevented from developing into a major one. Stairs should be safe and well lit as the elderly are sometimes unstable and often have poor eyesight. The elderly should always steady themselves by using both handrails. When ringing a doorbell, we should allow the elderly ample time to answer it, in case they are upstairs. If we become impatient and ring again without leaving a suitable pause, we might cause them to hurry or lose their concentration, and so be instrumental in causing them to fall.

To give just one example; an elderly woman fell on her way to answer the bell and injured herself so severely that she spent months in hospital. She and her husband had been about to move into a new home they had been saving for all their lives, and when they eventually did move in, after she was allowed out of hospital, two years were taken up with constant treatment as an out-patient at the local hospital where they taught her to walk again. During this time, her husband, who was older than herself, had to manage with all the housework, shopping and cooking. When, eventually they were able to go for a walk together, all she could manage were a few steps—and it remained that way, with their retirement ruined, because of a fall that need not have happened in the first place.

Steps, paths on the way to the dustbin, clothes lines, garden sheds, all can be dangerous, and it is a good idea to paint a white strip, or else use reflecting tape, along the top and edge of steps. This warns of a change of level. Always keep such areas clear of objects or garden tools which people might bump into. Watching someone knocked out by stepping on a garden rake, and being hit on the head by the handle, may be amusing when seen in a cartoon, but it is anything but funny when it happens to you.

During severe winter conditions, hospital casualty departments become choked with people who have slipped and fallen on icy steps, garden paths and pavements. Beware—people have severely injured themselves in the few steps it can take to fetch in the milk.

Steeplechasing, skiing, hang-gliding and parachuting all require specialist skills, and these qualities can be brought into use to enable people to walk in greater safety on frozen and slippery surfaces. One method, which works well, is to lean forward slightly and walk along on the balls of your feet. This shifts the centre of gravity, bringing it forward. Try it, gently and carefully at first, to see if it works for you. If it does, you may find that you can walk at a normal pace in perfect control, when everyone else is slipping all over the place.

Of course, ice and snow do not enter our homes, but many of the surfaces we expect people to walk on are just as slippery. Therefore, we should apply the same safeguards. Secure carpets and rugs by using a non-slip backing, and use non-slip floor polishes on all other floor surfaces. Wet surfaces in a bathroom or a kitchen should always be wiped dry immediately.

Any change from one type of floor covering to another should have the join covered with an aluminium strip to prevent the floor surface from curling up and tripping someone. Recessed doormats help to reduce accidents. If you are unable to have these fitted, make sure the doormat is kept in good condition and do not allow it to curl at the edges.

Specially designed non-slip rubber mats, often with suction pads underneath, help prevent falls in the shower or the bath, so do grab rails, and these are a must for the elderly and disabled. People fall when reaching for their towel after having a bath. Avoid this by making a point of placing it on a stool, or chair, close to the bath before you get in.

Brushes and brooms should be kept in cupboards, not underfoot; and electric flexes should never be left trailing, as they can be as lethal as trip wires. If we wake in the night, when our concentration and mental faculties are at their lowest ebb, and we need to leave the bedroom, a torch kept by the bed can help us make our way in safety.

Cots, prams, push-chairs and high-chairs may seem safe places to put infants, but a large number of serious falls result from people failing to use the safety harnesses properly, or through people purchasing unsafe equipment—such as cots without high enough sides and ends, or cots with bars spaced too far apart through which children can crawl or climb, often with fatal consequences, resulting from heads becoming jammed and children being hanged.

Falls from beds are common amongst all age groups, and infants should never be propped up in chairs or left unattended on beds. Even when placed in a carry-cot, it is vital that the carry-cot is placed on a firm base and cannot tip over in any circumstances.

Accidents happen because they are not expected—therefore they occur when we least expect them. A young woman fell to her death from a first floor window of her home in the south of England whilst waving goodbye to her parents.

Children left playing upstairs frequently fall from windows. The simple answer to this problem is to fit safety catches to the windows. These should open enough to allow for ventilation, but not enough to enable a child to climb or fall through. Safety bars that fit across windows are another alternative. Whichever alternative is used, the safety device must be capable of being removed quickly in the event of a fire.

Ladders used outside the
house should always be
angled safely at 70° to 75°
to the ground to prevent
slipping.

We put ourselves at risk every time we do something the easy way
rather than doing it the proper way. If we want to reach for something
from a shelf, clean the windows or do some decorating, what do we do?
We use a chair, or climb on the draining board, or stand on the banisters
to pull ourselves up into the loft—and many thousands of us end up in
hospital from an accident we could have avoided.

Safety-minded people, those who intend to keep out of hospital, use
household steps, or a ladder if they have to reach or work higher still.
Ladders and steps must be firm. Ladders used outside tend to slip if not
used correctly. The experts suggest placing the ladder at 70° to 75° to

Over-reaching is dangerous and likely to result in a loss of balance. It pays to climb down and re-position the ladder within comfortable reach of the work area.

the ground. There are attachments on the market which can be attached permanently to the base of a ladder, to enable it to be adjusted to suit any uneven ground or gradient, a universal joint also serves to provide an anti-slip footing.

Once up a ladder, there is always the temptation to reach out at arms length to carry out a job—do not do this. The only safe answer is to get down, move the ladder and climb it again. Always operate within a comfortable, easy reach of the work area. The need for stretching could so easily unbalance you.

Wooden ladders should be checked regularly to see that they are in good order. Metal ladders should last longer but there is one warning about metal ladders which must be given. Do not use them near electric equipment or overhead electric cables, you could get a shock and either be killed or severely burnt, or else thrown off the ladder, through your body being in contact with the metal ladder.

Reaching up for something we sometimes dislodge it. Falling objects cause accidents and it is usually the middle aged and the young who suffer most, with some of the mishaps proving fatal. Apart from causing cuts and bruises and more severe injuries, a falling object can lead to you falling as you hurriedly try to get out of its way. And thus you have a double accident. Place articles in safe positions where they are unlikely to fall, do not place them on top of loose cupboards which can be bumped into, or on shelves or furniture in rooms subject to vibration. The best place for heavy objects is at floor level, or in a cupboard fixed firmly to a wall.

FALL SAFE

Any one of us can fall at any time, even when we are fit, but we are far more likely to fall when we are tired, or when we are not concentrating, are run down, in a general low state of health, or elderly.

Since we are going to fall sometime we can lessen the risk of injury, or even avoid hurt altogether, if we know how to fall correctly. The secret is to relax; although this is easier said than done, particularly when falling downstairs. Nevertheless, the human body is capable of withstanding incredible knocks when totally relaxed, and this is why drunks usually get away with it.

Civilian parachutists and service paratroopers spend considerable time learning how to relax and land correctly. They have to learn this before they are allowed to make a jump. In some ways it is easier for them, because they know they are going to have to break their fall when landing and can prepare themselves. Whereas, when anyone falls by accident the fall happens without warning and has to be coped with instantly.

There are a couple of tips that can help us. Make sure you relax and let your body go limp. When falling feet first, absorb the shock by keeping your legs together and bending your knees, keep your elbows in and land on the balls of your feet. Roll over with any type of fall so that you take the brunt of the fall on the padded parts of your body, such as a shoulder, rather than on the bony and vulnerable areas. Carry the falls' momentum forward rather than stopping abruptly.

Of course, if a fall can be prevented by grabbing at some firm object, our first reactions should be concentrated on doing just this, but, if we are going to fall and there is no way of preventing it, we must do our best to relax and let our bodies go limp. It is the difference between pottery and damp clay. One shatters when dropped, the other absorbs the blow.

In some circumstances, the head may be the last part of the body to strike the ground. If you can keep your elbows in, and can reach up to protect your head with your hands, this is obviously a wise thing to do.

4

THE INVISIBLE PERILS OF GLASS

SHATTERING RESULTS

Few accidents are more tragic than those caused by glass. Just imagine for a moment ... a young husband is watching television in the sitting-room. His 28-year-old wife is busy in the kitchen and their two children are safely tucked up in bed. When the programme is over, he goes into the kitchen and finds his wife lying in a pool of blood on the floor—dead.

She had fallen through a glass door and the severe injuries caused by the dagger-shaped slivers of glass had caused her to bleed to death within minutes. The husband had been only yards away, yet he heard no breaking of glass, no scream, no shout for help.

Wherever you look in homes today, you will find glass being used. In large picture windows, in patio doors and double glazing. Inside the home you might find glass doors, partitions, low-level glass screens, bath and shower enclosures, and overhead glazing. Considering the wide use of glass, the accidents are statistically small in number, accounting for around 3% of home accidents. Statistics, however, can be misleading. 3% still adds up to 40,000 people who require medical treatment each year following glass accidents.

Accidents arise through people thinking a glass door is open when it is closed. This happened to a ten-year-old girl who ran through a patio door, slashing her head and severing an artery in two places. Luckily her mother was a trained nurse and acted immediately, applying pressure over the wound to reduce blood loss; otherwise the girl would have been dead within two minutes.

Although all age groups are at risk, the sad thing about these accidents is that the majority of victims are children or young people. Sadder still, when one realises that nearly every accident concerning glass could be avoided by taking certain precautions, or simply by installing safer glazing in the high risk areas around the house.

Serious accidents happen because people, especially children, think glass doors are open when they are not. Use 'safer glazing' materials—or make the glass obvious by fixing strong wooden bars across it or by marking it with paint, etching or motifs.

THE RISK AREAS

Most accidents happen in areas where there are glass doors, or doors with glass panels in them, or doors with glass surrounding them. Accidents also occur where there is low-level glazing in screens and partitions. The majority of these accidents are caused by children hurrying in these areas, perhaps during play, or by adults who are either unaware of the presence of glass, or else forget that it is there or accidentally fall into it even when they do know that it is there.

Dangers can arise when people visit your home or you go to theirs. This is particularly so with children. If it is fine, you might go into the garden through an opened patio door. Someone may close the door without telling you, or it may be blown shut by a gust of wind. If your children return to the house, because the glass is transparent, they might think the door is open, then find out too late that it is not.

DIFFERENT TYPES OF GLASS

Ordinary glass, described technically as *annealed* glass, but known by most of us as 'sheet glass', 'plate glass' or 'float glass', is used widely in homes, and if it is selected and installed in the correct way it is a perfectly satisfactory material. However, it is brittle and the risk of breakage and subsequent injury is high if it is installed unwisely.

For instance, it is dangerous to use too thin or too light-weight a glass in areas where people could come into violent contact with it. This is because annealed glass fractures, and produces comparatively large, razor-sharp fragments. These are often dagger-like in shape and can cause deep lacerations and other serious injuries.

'Figured rolled glass' is another form of annealed glass. This is either patterned or textured and is used in certain areas of the home to obscure vision. While it is more likely to be seen, it is still brittle. So the same selection and installation precautions apply. Avoid its use in panels at the bottom of stairs and in other high-risk areas.

In America, many of the States have passed laws insisting on the use of safety glass in high-risk areas. This has proved effective and has greatly reduced glass-related accidents. Experts in Britain and many other countries feel that they should follow this example, or at least point out the dangers and see that safety glass is specified for high-risk areas of glazing.

If you already have ordinary (annealed) glass in your home, and the chances are ten to one that you have, accidents can be avoided by making it abundantly clear where there is a pane of glass. For example, a bar, or bars, of strong wood put across a patio door (and painted if desired) will show when the door is closed. If, for some reason, anyone does happen to fall into the door, the barrier might prevent them from going right through the glass. Another alternative is to use motifs as markings, these can be transfers or stick-ons, butterflies, flowers etc.

It is a sensible precaution to make sure that areas that use glass are well illuminated. Also make sure that there is nothing near the glass which might contribute to people losing their balance and falling, such as electric flexes or loose rugs. Use opaque or translucent glass where it is not essential to be able to see through the panel.

Glass panels near doorways are often mistaken for doors. This can be prevented by guarding the panes with rails, or screening them with furniture, plants and flower troughs. Low-level windows can be protected by barrier rails, and children should be discouraged from playing near glazed areas.

Never push on glass to open a door or a window. Never slam windows, or bang on them to attract someone's attention.

If it is not practical to guard annealed glass in the risk areas, or if you want a large area of clear glass for an aesthetic reason, such as the need for greater light, or the view it gives, then one of the 'safer glazing' materials should be used. These include tempered (toughened) glass and laminated glass.

SAFER GLAZING MATERIALS

Tempered or *toughened* glass is made by taking ordinary annealed glass and putting it through a simple heat-treatment process. Without going into the technicalities of how this is done the end result is a sheet of glass up to five times tougher than the original annealed sheet.

In fact, a door or partition of fully-tempered glass of the appropriate thickness is so strong that a person running into it, or striking it with an outstretched arm, is most unlikely to break it.

Tempered glass is also *break-safe*, which means that if it does break under an exceptionally violent blow, the entire sheet shatters into thousands of small and relatively harmless pieces. This means the chances of cutting or piercing injuries are minimal.

This type of glass is recommended where the risks of accidental impact are high, such as large panels in doors, glass surrounding doors, and low-level glazing. Also use this for shower and bath enclosures as there is always the risk of someone slipping.

LAMINATED GLASS

This is made by inserting a sheet of resilient plastic between sheets of glass and then bonding together under heat and pressure.

Laminated glass also possesses break-safe properties, but in a different way to toughened glass. A sufficiently strong blow against a laminated glass will crack the outside sheets of glass. The panel, however, will remain in one piece, with the tough plastic interlayer holding the cracked fragments together. This virtually does away with the risks of laceration.

Tempered and laminated glass should be used with furniture, shelves, table tops etc. It can also be used in double-glazing.

PLASTIC

Modern technology has come up with various plastic materials which can be used instead of glass. These are available as clear, patterned or tinted plastic sheets of various thicknesses.

Acrylic sheet has greater impact resistance than tempered or laminated glass, and it can be used to replace glass in doors and low-level glazing, shower and bath enclosures.

Polycarbonate sheet is the strongest transparent material and is virtually unbreakable when used for glazing.

Because of their higher cost, both materials are used chiefly for security purposes, such as jewellers' windows and anti-vandal screens, but they can equally well be specified for high-risk areas in the home.

As plastic materials are less resistant to scratching than glass, they will lose their surface brilliance after some time in use.

SAFE CHOICE

Although safer glazing materials may cost more to purchase, they cost no more than glass to install, and once put in they are much less likely to be broken. For anyone buying a new house, the difference in cost between safe and unsafe glazing is negligible.

If safer glazing materials were used in high-risk areas in houses, almost every glass-related accident could be prevented.

It is worth stressing that when ordinary (annealed) glass shatters, its dagger-like slivers can cause death, or injuries that result in handicaps and scarring for life. No one wants that to happen in their home or in a home that they are visiting. Research shows that people *are* prepared to pay for safety if the benefits are explained to them.

5

ELECTRICAL SAFETY

The surface of our planet must have seemed an inhospitable place to our early ancestors. Particularly when we realise that the energy dissipated in one lightning strike is greater than the output of a modern power station. Trees that had been set alight probably provided them with their first source of fire, which virtually makes the caveman the earliest user of electricity.

Electricity to provide heat, light and power in our homes is a development which has taken place over the last 100 years. Today it is in such widespread use in so many different ways, making life easier, more comfortable and enjoyable, that we tend to take it for granted.

Electricity is a wonderful servant—but a dangerous master. If used or installed incorrectly or tampered with it can kill. One of the difficulties is that our five senses are unable to alert us to the danger, for we cannot see, hear or smell electric current, and we certainly cannot taste it, and if we touch it or come into contact with it accidentally, it can be lethal!

Many people think it is only the very high voltages in the power-line transmission cables that can kill. That is incorrect. Even a few milliamps through the muscles of the heart are sufficient to stun it and stop it beating under certain circumstances.

The low voltage used in house current—240 volts in Britain and 230 volts in many Commonwealth countries, 220 volts in Europe (sometimes 110 volts), and 110 volts in America and Canada—can cause extremely unpleasant shocks, or worse, prove lethal. Electricity must be treated with respect and understanding, only then will it continue to serve us.

It is not uncommon for the average home to have at least a dozen different electrical appliances. See how many you have:

Electric cooker	Garden pool lighting
Frying pan	Fountain
Casserole	Storage heater

Microwave oven
Griller or spit-roaster
Toaster
Tea maker
Refrigerator
Food freezer
Kettle
Coffee grinder
Percolator
Food mixer
Liquidiser
Carving knife
Dishwasher
Vacuum cleaner
Floor polisher
Carpet shampooer
Extractor fan
Cooling fan
Air conditioning unit
Razor
Toothbrush
Hair dryer
Hair curler
Sewing machine
Typewriter
Lawnmower
Hedgetrimmer
Garden shears
Greenhouse heater
Garden lighting

Radiant heater
Convector heater
Fan heater
Oil-filled radiator
Immersion heater
Over-sink water heater
Water pump
Shower pack unit
Washing machine
Spin drier
Tumble drier
Clothes drier
Iron
Electric blanket
Lights
Standard lamp
Table lamp
Infra-red lamp
Ultra-violet lamp
Clock
Television
Record player
Radio
Film projector
Slide projector
Tape recorder
DIY power tools
Drill
Electric saw etc.

This list is far from complete and no doubt you can think of some more, but it does show that electricity is something we have to learn to *live* with.

The important thing to remember is that electricity always seeks the easiest and quickest route to the earth. If something is wrong, the shortest path could be through us. Shocks are all too common, although, fortunately, fatal accidents are rare. However, electric shocks, even when non-fatal, can often result in severe burns. We should also remember that a high proportion of all fires are due to electrical causes, such as the deterioration, neglect, or misuse of electrical appliances and installations. Yet, virtually all electrical accidents could be avoided!

DOMESTIC WIRING SYSTEMS

To regard users of electricity as 'consumers' is misleading, because electricity is not consumed, rather, its energy is harnessed to provide light, warmth and power in our homes. A brief description of the domestic wiring system should clear up any confusion. The wiring system should consist of three wires. The *live* wire carries electricity from the generator at the power station, and the *neutral* wire takes it back. The third wire, known as the *earth* wire, serves as the vital *safety* wire, by taking the current safely to earth if a short circuit should occur. This can happen if the *live* wire touches the frame of an appliance. Instead of the current passing through us, the circuit is completed via the *earth* wire.

For safety reasons it is important to ensure that any electrical installation in your house is carried out by a qualified electrician. If the wiring is more than 25 years old, or if the socket outlets have *round* 2-pin or 3-pin and are thus unshuttered, which means the holes are open and present a potential hazard to children poking around, then the whole wiring circuit will be outdated and will almost certainly need to be renewed.

In many homes the earth connections were made to water pipes. This earthing should be checked because plastic piping may have been used in sections which have been replaced or added to, thus breaking the continuity of the earthing system. In any event, even in newer houses, it is always wise to have all the wiring checked every five years. Particular attention should be paid to the earthing system.

If you discover, or suspect, a fault in the house wiring, or in an electrical appliance, do not try to repair it yourself. It is far safer to call in a specialist. Amateur work can be extremely dangerous. In some countries the law forbids it and will not even allow a householder to wire a plug.

One way of getting an electric shock is to come into contact with an appliance which is faulty and unearthed. This is why a plug must never be pulled from a socket by its flex. If you do this, the wires inside can work loose without you knowing it, and can touch and so cause a short circuit, possibly a fire, or, in cases where the earth wire has become disconnected, result in electrocution. A 14-month-old boy was killed when his metal high-chair touched an electrical refrigerator. An earth wire in the plug had worked loose and made the fridge 'live'.

PLUG IN TO SAFETY

A plug is just a plug to most people—but electrical appliances operate at different wattages (marked on them) and need to be correctly wired and fused. It never pays to buy cheap plugs. In Britain it is estimated that out of the 400 million plugs in use over 70 million could be faulty

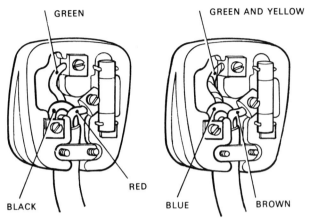

GREEN

GREEN AND YELLOW

RED

BLACK

BLUE

BROWN

Old wiring colour code. Green lead to earth terminal (marked 'E' on most plugs). Black to neutral 'N'. Red to live terminal 'L'.

New wiring colour code. Green/yellow lead to earth terminal 'E'. Blue to neutral terminal 'N'. Brown to live terminal 'L'.

Note: if there are only two leads they must be connected to the 'L' and 'N' terminals—never to the 'E' (earth) terminal.

and might prove lethal.

The only safe answer is to buy plugs from a reputable source, and to seek advice from the official electrical authority or from a fully qualified electrician. Having bought your plug, it now needs to be wired correctly and it is surprising how few people know how to do this.

When you buy an appliance from an electrical shop it saves time and trouble, and is far safer, if you ask them to wire it for you. Having wired it, a conscientious electrician will use a test-meter to check that everything is correct.

HOW TO WIRE A PLUG

If, on the other hand, you decide to or if you have to, wire a plug, it is essential that you know precisely how this should be done. A survey has shown that a large number of adults still do not know how to do this. Make sure you get it right and if you have any difficulties or doubts, stop what you are doing and get expert advice.

An international colour coding is now in use but in the past different countries identified the earth, live and neutral wires with different colour codes, often using different names to describe them. There are still appliances in use with the old colour codes, and it is vital to seek expert advice to see that these are connected correctly and securely.

Modern plugs have three flat pins, with the plug containing a fuse, designed for use with 13 amp socket outlets in Britain. The flexes for modern appliances have three leads. Each lead is a different colour. The blue wire should be connected to the neutral (N) terminal in the plug, brown to live (L) and yellow/green to earth (E). This is the new colour code introduced in recent years. Old appliances might have the old colour coding with the black flex being connected to the neutral terminal, red to live and green to earth.

To wire a plug you will need a screwdriver and a sharp knife to cut the wires to the required length or, better still, a wire stripper which cuts through the insulation and strips it away without damaging the wires.

For plugs with the new colour coding, the first thing to do is unscrew the plug top, then remove the cartridge fuse. If you are unable to remove it with your fingers, use a small screwdriver to gently lever it out. As you look at the open back of the plug, holding it with the flex or cable entry point at the bottom, the earth pin (E) will be at the top centre, the live pin (L) at bottom right, and the neutral pin (N) at the bottom left. At the lower edge of the plug you should notice a grip that is used to secure the flex coming from the appliance. Some plugs use a fibrous bar held by two screws. Loosen one screw, remove the other and swing the bar clear. There are other forms of cable grip, the most common being a V shape made from two strips of plastic which grip the cable by squeezing to secure it. If your plug has one of these V-shaped grips, you will have to push the wire into it later.

Carefully cut away 2 in. (50 mm) of the flex's outer sheath, leaving the three rubber covered wires intact and making sure you do not cut through their rubber. This needs to be done very gently if you are using a knife, otherwise you could cut through the insulation of the wires without noticing the cuts in the rubber. This could be dangerous and might later cause a short circuit or result in the appliance becoming live. It is best to use wire strippers made for the job, these are, or can be, pre-set to cut and strip away the required amount without error. If you use a knife, it pays when finished to grip the three inner wires in one hand and pull the outer covering of the flex in the opposite direction, so you can then check that the insulation on the three inner wires has not been cut. Only pull back fractionally, then when you let go the outer sheath will slide back into place. If the inner rubber has been accidentally cut, sever the three wires at that point and start again. It will shorten the flex by 2 in. (5 cm) but a shorter flex is better than a shortened life.

Put the flex into the plug with the outer covering of the flex positioned

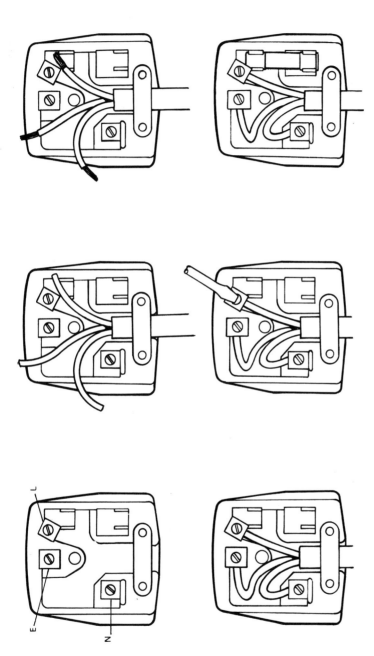

It is vital for everyone's safety that plugs are wired and fused correctly. For the old and new wiring colour codes see the diagrams on page 65. For full details see PLUG IN TO SAFETY (page 64), HOW TO WIRE A PLUG (page 65) and CORRECT FUSES (page 69). See pages 18 and 69 for precise fuse ratings for different appliances.

beyond the grip which will hold it in position, this lets you judge how long the three wires need to be to reach their terminals. Some people prefer to fasten the flex sheath firmly under the clamp at this stage. Whether you do so now or later, you will see that the green/yellow earth wire will need to be longer than the others as it has further to reach. As a precaution, give the earth wire a little extra slack, so that if appliances such as irons or vacuum cleaners are tugged at any time, the vital earth wire on the plug end of the flex will not be pulled out of its terminal.

Trim the insulation covering of each wire to expose about ¼ in. (6 mm) of wire for screwhole terminals, or about ½ in. (13 mm) for clamp type terminals. Do not cut more insulation than this, otherwise one bare wire might touch another inside the plug. Be careful not to cut any of the strands of the wires inside either, this could lead to overloading and heating, through insufficient wire being available to carry the current.

Twist the strands of each wire so they form a smooth end without any stray whiskers, then insert into the correct terminals. *New colour code*, green/yellow wire to the earth terminal (marked E on most plugs), blue wire to the neutral terminal (N) and the brown wire to the live terminal (L). In the *old colour code*, it would be green to the earth terminal, black to neutral and red to live.

Having done this, tighten the screws and make sure that they are tight and cannot work loose (remember the little boy electrocuted in his highchair). If the terminals are the clamp type, loop the wires in a *clockwise* direction around the terminals, so that when you screw down the wires will not be unwound but will be firmly secured.

Next fit the correct fuse into position, then have another look to see that all three wires are *connected* to their correct terminals and are *secure*. Fasten the appliance cable firmly in place under the bar grip, if you did not choose to do so earlier. Either tighten the screws on each side of it, or press the cable firmly in place between the V-shaped strips of plastic if the plug is fitted with a squeeze grip. However the cable is secured, make sure the clamping device grips the outer sheath and not just the leads. Now refit the cover. There are some household plugs available in which the grip tightens when any strain is applied to the cord, and in which the live pins are partly covered by insulating sleeves to prevent accidental contact if the plug is pulled partially out of its socket. This is an important safeguard against prying fingers when there are children around. One particular make of plug incorporates an additional sensible feature in that inside the plug all three terminals are the same distance from the cord grip, so that all three wires can be cut to the same length.

Plugs should be checked regularly. Screws can work loose, so it is important that all the wires are in their correct positions and that the screws are still tight. The condition of the plug should also be checked, in case it has become chipped or cracked. If it has, it should be replaced.

Some electrical appliances are *double-insulated* or *all-insulated*. There is no need for these terms to mystify people. Without going into technical details, it means that the earthing is taken care of within the appliance and so these particular appliances only require a 2-core flex which can be wired to a 3-pin plug using the live and neutral terminals. Ignore the earth terminal in the plug. When you buy one of these double-insulated or all-insulated appliances, make a point of reading the manufacturer's instructions about their correct wiring and use. They are often portable and they should never be allowed to get wet, as this can interfere with the specially devised insulation of the electrical parts inside.

These modern tools give excellent service, but there are some old domestic appliances which have 2-core flexes but are *not* double-insulated or all-insulated. For that matter they are not properly insulated at all, so avoid using them or purchasing them second-hand as they are dangerous if a fault occurs.

A high proportion of all fires are attributed to electrical causes through the neglect or misuse of appliances and installations. Various safeguards have been included in the chapter on *Fire* under the sub-heading KEEP-ING ELECTRICITY UNDER CONTROL.

CORRECT FUSES
Reference has been made to *miniature circuit breakers* (M.C.B.) fitted at the mains distribution board as an alternative to fuses. These operate automatically and break the circuit when there is an overload of current. When tripped they can be reset by pressing a button. If the fault in the circuit remains the circuit breaker immediately breaks the circuit again.

A more recent innovation is known as an *earth leakage circuit breaker* (E.L.C.B.) which is more sensitive and operates quickly. There are usually two E.L.C.B.s, one for the lighting circuit and one for the sockets throughout the house. Some of the earlier *voltage-operated* E.L.C.B.s proved unsatisfactory. So, if you are having one fitted, the experts recommend the later *current-operated* E.L.C.B.s which operate safely and eliminate the hazards.

Where wired fuses or cartridge fuses are used for the mains, it is vital that the correct fuses are fitted for the different circuits. If you fit a fuse which is rated too highly, the fuse may not blow and you could get a shock, or it might cause a fire. When you buy a 13 amp plug it will most likely have a 13 amp cartridge fuse already fitted inside. Many appliances use a 3 amp fuse, so you will need to take the 13 amp fuse out of the plug and change to the lower rating. In any event, the appliance manufacturer's instructions should tell you which fuse to use.

Details about mains fuses are given in the *Fire* chapter (p 18) which also deals with how to replace wired and cartridged fuses. You will need 5 amp fuses for lighting circuits, 15 or 20 amp fuses for immersion heaters, 30 amp fuses for ring main circuits, and 45 amp fuses for electric cookers. You will also need 3 amp and 13 amp fuses for use in plugs.

DANGERS OF OVERLOADING

Also mentioned are the dangers of overloading through using too many appliances from an adaptor placed in a single socket. Ideally, there should be a separate socket outlet for every appliance. If you make a habit of using two appliances from one point, you will find it more convenient and much safer to have the single socket replaced by a double socket.

Advice is given on the correct use of flexes and use of the right wattage bulb for a particular type of shade—together with a great deal of general information on the purchase and safe use of electric blankets.

WATER AND ELECTRICITY—A LETHAL COMBINATION

Most of us know that water conducts electricity and that water and electricity are a deadly combination. Yet people still put flower vases or goldfish bowls on top of the television set. Never do this—and always be careful to dry your hands before you touch switches, plugs, or any electrical appliances. The addition of liquid increases your chance of being electrocuted and means that even a small shock might prove fatal. This is why portable electrical appliances must never be taken into the bathroom, even if plugged in outside. If you have an electric heater, make sure that it is wall-mounted, permanently wired in, and fitted with a cord which you pull to switch it on or off. The heater must be away from the bath or basin and must be sited high on the wall where you cannot reach or touch it.

The light should also be operated by a pull cord, as should mirror lights if you use them. The main bathroom light should be fitted with a protective skirt to make sure the metal parts of the lamp or bulb cannot be touched. It should only be used as a light, never plug a hair drier or a radio or anything else into it.

There should not be any socket outlets in the bathroom. The only exception is the special permanent socket outlet for an electric shaver. This is designed with special safety features—but be careful even when using this. Make sure your face and hands are dry and do not shave with water in the basin. Shavers have been dropped into basins and have elec-

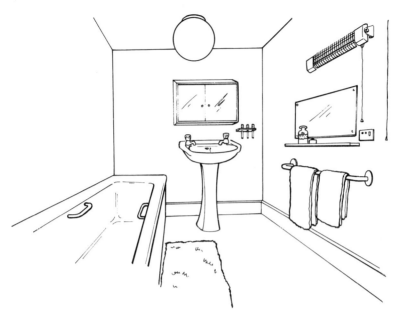

Electrical appliances must never be taken into the bathroom, even if plugged in from outside. Heaters must be permanently wired in and must be operated by pull cords. Heaters must be wall mounted away from bath, shower or basin. Shavers must only be used with a special permanent shaver socket with an approved isolating transformer. All lights in a bathroom must be operated by pull cords.

trocuted people who tried to retrieve them without first disconnecting the shavers from the power supply. The shaver-sockets should be sited to prevent users from touching taps or metal water pipes and basins, but as the cords attached to most electric shavers are coiled and can be extended by pulling, this is where the dangers can arise. So shave opposite the socket position keeping away from the basin and other danger areas.

So many tragedies occur through people ignoring these safety precautions. A faulty and incorrectly sited radiant heater electrocuted a woman who stood up in the bath to adjust the angle of the reflector. A teenage girl was killed when a radio which was plugged in outside the bathroom fell into her bath. A seven-year-old girl was killed when her father brought a table lamp into the bathroom because the bathroom light had failed. The lamp fell off the window ledge into the bath and electrocuted the child. These are not just isolated incidents. Newspapers regularly contain such accounts. So make certain your bathroom is safe and that the safety rules are always followed. These rules apply anywhere water is used.

A word of warning must be given about downstairs lavatories. These often contain basins, with light switches installed on the wall within a few feet of the basin. Make sure your hands are dry before you operate the switch, or, better still, get an electrician to install a ceiling mounted pull cord switch to replace the wall switch.

The kitchen is another danger area. Electric sockets and switches are frequently mounted on the wall. Once again, never touch them unless you have dried your hands first. Make sure the floors are dry before touching a switch or using an electrical appliance—and watch out for spillages from such equipment as washing machines.

Everyone loves a bargain, but purchasing second-hand electrical appliances is unwise and can be dangerous. Cables and flexes are frequently patched with insulating tape. If the tape is removed, a wire is usually found to be bare, and this could prove fatal, particularly with washing machines or other appliances which use water. Cables and flexes should never be patched up with insulating tape, the whole cable should be renewed. Second-hand equipment sometimes has a 2-core flex without a safety earth wire—and the earthing on the appliances and plugs is often faulty.

USING ELECTRICITY SAFELY IN THE KITCHEN

The kitchen is the work centre of the home and, as such, the place where most electrical appliances are used. If we start with the cooker the first thing is to make sure no flexes ever trail across the top. Check that the cooker is switched off at the control panel before you clean it. If you use kitchen foil, keep it away from the grill elements and never line the oven or any other part of the cooker with it.

All electrical appliances should be switched off and unplugged before cleaning. They should also be unplugged when not in use.

When using a kettle always make sure the element is covered with water before switching on, even if you are only making one cup of tea. At the other extreme, do not overfill the kettle; and always switch off and unplug the kettle at the wall before filling or pouring.

If a toaster becomes obstructed, switch it off and unplug it. Even then do not use a metal tool. Let the toaster cool then gently remove the bread with a wooden tool avoiding the heating elements which can become damaged.

If you have a bayonet-type adaptor in your home—you shouldn't have! They are outdated and extremely dangerous, as electric irons and other appliances need to be earthed and require a 3-core flex and a 3-pin plug,

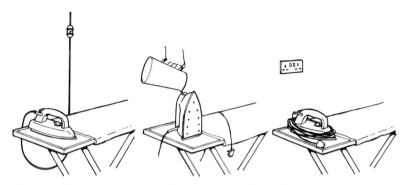

Electric appliances must never be run from a lamp fitting. Electric irons and other appliances need to be earthed and require a 3-core flex, a correctly fused 3-pin plug and a wall socket. The floor should be dry when ironing. Steam irons must be switched off and unplugged before filling.
Never coil the flex around a hot iron, as this could ruin the insulation around the wires. Let the iron cool before coiling the flex around the iron and putting it away.

and should, therefore, never be used from lamp fittings.

Make sure the floor is not wet when ironing. If you use a steam iron always switch it off and unplug it before filling it with water. When you have finished ironing, do not coil the flex around the hot iron or you will ruin the insulation around the wires, and this might lead to a shock when you next use it. Let the iron cool before putting it away.

MAKING A CHANGE

More and more people are buying or renting new houses or flats, changing homes, or making changes or additions to existing ones. This means we are constantly buying new electrical equipment. So we need to be on our guard more than ever before. If, for example, any of your plugs or sockets become warm during use, they are warning you of a fault that could lead to a fire, or could lead to someone getting a shock. Get an expert in to check it—experts cost money, but faults can cost lives.

Modern sockets are shuttered for safety, but if your sockets are not shuttered, you can buy special plugs that go in the sockets when the sockets are not in use, to prevent children from poking their fingers into the holes. Turn off the electricity at the switch when overhead electric light bulbs need changing. Switch off table or standard lamps at the socket and remove the plug before you change a bulb. Allow time for bulbs to cool before removing them. Overhead lights should be switched off before you clean their lampshades, and lamps should be unplugged.

People have been electrocuted or severely burnt when putting bare wires into sockets. Appliances must never be used without plugs.

RENOVATIONS
Renovations need to be carried out with care. A builder using a hammer and chisel on an old cottage wall, because he wanted to remove and renew a section suffering from excessive damp, struck the electric wiring. In this particular case, because he was on a wooden floor, it was non-fatal, but with concrete or other types of floor he could easily have been killed. Turn off the electricity at the mains before using a hammer and chisel on the wall. The same applies when using nails, pins or picture hooks. It is impossible to know where the electric wires run inside the walls, and we could so easily strike them.

If we are drilling holes in the walls, we should remove the relevant lighting and power fuses at the mains, after switching off the mains before doing so, only then should we use a hand drill. If we need to use a power-drill, the supply must come from an area of the house where the electricity has not been switched off, in which case a safety-approved extension lead will be needed.

POWER CUTS
There are times when the electricity supply to your home may be interrupted. When this happens, switch off all electrical appliances and move all heaters away from furniture and furnishings. Leave at least one light on so you will know when the power has been restored. If the cut is a long one and you decide to go to bed, the switched off appliances will avoid the risk of fire. When the power is restored, do not forget to adjust the time control on the central heating boiler, if you have one.

ELECTRICITY OUT OF DOORS
The safety rules for within the home apply to the use of electrical equipment outside it. Garages or workshops usually have concrete floors which, like water, act as conductors of electricity. It is safest to work on wooden boards.

Exertion makes people sweat, and moist skin increases the dangers of an electric shock. So electric tools should have properly installed and earthed 3-pin sockets. They must never be run from a lamp socket. Protected lead-lamps should be used—and all portable power-operated tools should be of an approved type and from a reliable manufacturer. Some of these are all-insulated or double-insulated for maximum safety.

Care must be taken when using electric mowers, hedge trimmers and other appliances, not to cut through the cable. All tools must be switched off, with the plug disconnected from the socket, before blades or cutters are cleaned or adjusted.

If extension leads are used, they should be purchased ready assembled, or be made up by a qualified electrician. The flex must be single and continuous, without joins, and it must never be wet or worn.

Some people floodlight their gardens, or pools and also operate fountains. This work must be carried out by an expert.

Some householders have large gardens, others have small gardens, some have no gardens at all. There are hazards in all these situations. Bunting is frequently put up during national celebrations and carnival weeks and other local festivities. Danger arises when the bunting is fixed to poles carrying live and potentially lethal electric lines.

A man was killed as he stood on a ladder outside his house and tried to throw bunting over a 415 volt electric mains. He lost his balance and grabbed hold of the wire. There was a bang and a flash and the man's seven-year-old son watched as his father crashed to the ground, killed instantly.

AVOIDING HAZARDS OVERHEAD

The overhead wires bringing electricity to our homes are safe—until anyone touches them. If touched, or if they come into contact with long metal poles or rods or certain other objects, they can kill. Anyone who flies kites or model aeroplanes should take great care, and should try to imagine that they are flying real machines. Real aeroplanes are controlled before being cleared for take off, during flight, and while landing. Children and their parents should observe the same safety rules and should make sure they are well away from electrical sub-stations, pylons and overhead power lines. What you may not realise is that, even if made of string or nylon, kite or model control lines can become conductors of electricity. They are even more dangerous if wet or if they are moist after touching the ground.

Failure to observe the safety rules and keep clear of transmission lines and electrical equipment can result in burns, electrocution, or death. Make sure the area is clear if you want to stay safe.

Tell children that if ever they do see their kite or model areoplane about to go into an overhead line, they should *let go*. Once it is lodged in the line, they should make no attempt to retrieve their plaything, either by poking at it, throwing things at it, or climbing poles or pylons. Kites and model aeroplanes are expensive toys, but your children will not live long enough to make another flight if they ignore these warnings.

If a kite or aeroplane gets lodged in the overhead cables, you or your children must not touch the strings or any other part of the kite or aero-

Kites and model aeroplanes must never be flown near overhead power cables. String and nylon control lines can become conductors of electricity, especially if wet or slightly moist from touching the ground—and this can result in electrocution or severe burns.

plane. Contact the electricity authority, they are the *only* people who can disentangle it for you. The same applies to free-flying model aeroplanes and gliders if they get stuck. Phone for the police (dial 999 in Britain) and they will contact the electricity authority. Everyone should keep their distance from the spot. If there is a short to earth—the ground nearby could become 'live'.

It may seem far fetched to bring in the next piece of advice, but it is something which *does* cause concern, particularly to Air Sea Rescue helicopter crews. The Air Navigation Orders state that no kite-flying is permitted within 5 nautical miles of an airfield. Apparently, some children do fly their kites from gardens and housing estates near runways. Even beyond that distance, kite-flying is limited to a height of 170 feet (51 metres). This presents problems along the coast, particularly when there are off-shore winds to take the kites over the sea. It is very difficult to see a kite from a helicopter. If a helicopter does get tangled with a kite, it can be dangerous; even more so if the dangling lines happen to touch high-voltage cables. In any event, an Air Sea Rescue helicopter is there on a mission to save lives, and they often need to fly low along the shortest route to save vital seconds—extra hazards are something they can do without.

Bird-nesting is another hobby which concerns the electrical authorities. They point out that as birds can sometimes nest safely in 'live' equipment, this gives a false impression that the wires are safe to touch and attracts bird-nesting children. What is overlooked, is that many birds are electrocuted when they make the mistake of spreading their wings. If they touch a wire and earth wire, the current passes through their bodies. Children are obviously at risk if they climb poles or pylons, they can also be at risk if they climb a tree to reach a bird's nest. In one case, a branch swayed and touched an overhead wire, there was a flash and the explosion killed the boy instantly. Apart from the dangers, thoughtless egg-stealing depletes wildlife stock.

Domestic animals trapped up electricity poles or in trees near power lines are another problem. Children become distraught when they see their pets in this situation, and their natural reaction makes them try to do something about it. One little girl persuaded a soldier to rescue a cat. He put a ladder against the pole, and almost electrocuted himself. In this case the electricity did not 'lock him on', but threw him to the ground and he recovered after a night in hospital. Call the electrical authority, never try to rescue the animal yourself.

One point that needs stressing is that children see engineers working on overhead lines and they think this means those lines are safe to touch. They do not realise that the engineers have turned off the supply and earthed down the lines before working on them.

Children also see engineers reach up and touch high-voltage lines with rods. These are specially manufactured (live line) rods which are fully insulated and are issued only to the engineers, because they know how to use them.

Remember, electricity is a faithful servant, but a dangerous master if used or installed incorrectly, or tampered with. Overhead lines are an essential part of life, for without them, particularly in rural areas, many people would have no electricity. Having electricity in the home, we should always treat it with respect, use it wisely and observe the safety rules. People *do* live to a ripe old age. We can too, if we take care, because electrical accidents are nearly always avoidable.

6

HAZARDS IN THE GARDEN

MOWING THE LAWN

A high proportion of all accidents occur in the garden, in garden sheds and in the garage, and the causes are less obvious than you might imagine. Take mowing for instance. Despite warnings and safety instructions, many people underestimate how deadly power mowers can be. The sharp metal blade of the mower revolves about 4,000 times a minute and can hurl pieces of glass and stone at speeds of up to 170 mph (275 kph).

Who would have believed that an accident could be caused inside a home by someone mowing outside it? But this happened. A power mower sent a loose stone flying across the garden from a considerable distance, it went through a glass window and struck a woman in a room inside the house and killed her.

All mowers should be treated with respect. Before you start cutting the grass you should walk round the lawn picking up loose stones, glass, twigs, nails, bits of wire and other objects. Always wear gloves and sensible shoes when mowing and never mow the lawn in sandals or bare feet. There have been an alarming number of mowing accidents in Britain and North America that have led to amputations being performed during hospital treatment.

Petrol mowers must be filled in the open, never in a shed or a garage because of the danger from explosive fumes which can cover a wide area —make sure the sparking plug cable has been disconnected before you fill the mower. Mowers have been known to start automatically when their blades have been turned. The same precautions apply if you are refuelling during mowing. Stop the engine and disconnect the spark plug.

Electric mowers must always be turned off at the mains and unplugged and disconnected from the supply before you attempt any adjustments.

Sometimes people trail the electric flex through the front door. A gust of wind can blow a door shut and damage or sever a cable, so use a door-stop. If the front door needs to be shut to keep draughts out or keep the children in, then feed the flex through your letter box. But be

Always switch off and unplug electric mowers and hedgetrimmers before touching the blades or cutters to clean them, make adjustments or clear obstructions.

sure to have a key handy so you can get back in, if you need to switch off the power supply.

Special care must be taken when there are children around. It is safest to keep them indoors. Children should never be allowed to touch or use mowers (mowers should never be left running *or* unattended), and they should never be given rides on them. Many children have been killed or injured after tumbling off a mower.

If there is a slope, the safe way to mow it is sideways along the slope—never up and down the incline. But be careful that the mower does not overturn sideways—if the slope is very steep you will have to cut the grass by hand!

OTHER POWER AND HAND TOOLS

Electric mowers must never be used when the grass is wet or when it is raining, neither must hedgetrimmers or other electrical appliances. Concentration is required when an appliance is used. So many accidents happen when someone's attention is diverted. Cables must be kept clear of the cutters. When hedge-trimming, never overreach, particularly if using a step ladder, and make sure you avoid items of loose clothing that can become entangled in the cutting blades.

If something blocks or jams the blades, disconnect the hedgetrimmer before you attempt to remove the cause of obstruction. That way you will be safe and still retain the number of fingers you started with.

Watch how swiftly a chain-saw cuts through a tree and you will realise that its use requires care and concentration.

It is not only power-operated garden tools that cause accidents, hand-operated tools can be just as dangerous if misused or used unwisely. Rakes, hoes, brooms and similar garden tools can be dangerous if left lying around, instead of being hung up or stored away. They can trip someone or can cause a serious injury to anyone treading on them.

EYE INJURIES
Injuries can occur when you stoop to tend a flower or plant, through a twig or thorn piercing an eye. If you injure an eye, seek immediate medical attention from a doctor or hospital. It is better to be safe than sorry, and if you ignore a slight injury it could lead to the loss of sight or impaired vision.

BEWARE OF POISONS
Children enjoy being in the garden and they have every right to expect it to be a safe place in which to play. So it is up to adults to see that all the dangers are removed. Poisoning comes high on the list of hazards, but the risk can be eliminated if we treat all garden chemicals, fertilisers, insecticides and pesticides as being potentially lethal and keep them locked away, well out of the reach of children. A child does not necessarily have to swallow any of these products to be poisoned. Some of the chemicals can kill if they are inhaled or absorbed through the skin. Empty containers must also be disposed of where children cannot get at them, and bait for vermin and other pests must never be placed where children can find it.

POISONOUS PLANTS
There are many plants which can poison and sometimes kill people or make them extremely ill. The *deadly nightshade* berry immediately springs to mind as does *laburnum* whose pealike pods attract children as they tend to look like food. *Laburnum* seeds have been responsible

DEADLY NIGHTSHADE   LABURNUM   YEW

Children should be warned never to eat anything they find growing in the garden or elsewhere. Deadly nightshade, laburnum and yew are just three among hundreds of poisonous plants, shrubs, trees and fungi.

for a number of cases of poisoning, some proving fatal. A *laburnum* tree in full flower is a beautiful addition to any garden, and the solution is to remove the pods after flowering and burn them. An adult must be present while this is being done. Pods must never be put on a rubbish tip. Where there are large trees, it is not easy to remove all the pods, so children should be warned never to touch pods when they fall.

The seeds of *larkspur, lupin, broom* and *wisteria* can also be dangerous. So too can certain bulbs, so the answer is to keep all bulbs away from children.

Leaves look harmless enough—but those of the *foxglove, lily of the valley* and *poinsettia* can kill if chewed or swallowed.

At Christmas be sure the *mistletoe* is hung safely. If children or adults eat the berries they can be killed. Any berries that drop to the floor must be picked up immediately and burnt or flushed down the lavatory. *Holly* berries can cause severe stomach upsets. Pigs thrive on *acorns*, but horses die from eating them. Children should never be allowed to put them in their mouths.

The answer as far as children are concerned is to warn them never to suck or eat anything they find in the garden.

The list of poisonous plants and fungi runs into hundreds, and, unless we are trained botanists, it is hard to identify the hazards and know what is dangerous and should be removed from our gardens at all costs, and what can be left quite safely. Any one of a number of specialist books will help, for example see *Poisonous Plants and Fungi in Colour* by Pamela North, Blandford Press.

HIDDEN DANGERS IN THE SOIL
Soil can also contain hazards and children are at risk when they play, crawl or roll over on the ground. If children swallow soil or put their fingers in their mouths some of the organisms they ingest are bound to be dangerous. Others are able to enter the body through wounds. A jab from a garden fork, a prick from a thorn, a bite or a scratch from an animal, they can all be sufficient to allow infected organisms into the blood. The spores of certain soil organisms which pass into the blood and cause tetanus can prove fatal unless the victim receives immediate medical treatment.

It is wise for adults to use a barrier cream and effective gloves when working in the garden. Tell children about the dangers of getting soil, or putting fingers, in their mouths. Existing cuts or wounds should be protected with sterile waterproof dressings. Warn children that they must tell you if they cut themselves or damage their skin while playing in the garden. That way you can clean the wound, using soap and water and washing outwards from the wound to avoid contamination. Then apply a dressing. If you suspect infection, get medical attention at once, an anti-tetanus injection might be required.

SAFE FOR CHILDREN

There are hundreds of other things to be considered to enable children to play in safety in the garden. For a start, we need to keep them in the garden, so fencing should be in good condition and there should be child-proof safety catches on the gates.

Lily ponds and goldfish ponds need fencing or netting to prevent children from falling into them. A 22-month-old boy drowned in 2 ft (·6 m) of water while staying at the farmhouse of a friend of his parents. This particular story happened to make the headlines, but we seldom hear about more than a fraction of the tragedies and deaths that happen each year. Water butts and tanks can be dangerous and should be covered, and children should never be left on their own near swimming pools.

Even if you have no pets, do use a pram safety net when putting infants out in the garden.

Ornamental pools need fencing to prevent children from falling into them. People can drown in only a few inches of water so never leave children by themselves near any kind of pool, including swimming pools.

The hard-edged seats of swings cause hundreds of accidents each year by striking children's heads. If you have a swing in your garden, edge it with soft, round-edged, shock-absorbent material. One of the safest and cheapest ways of doing this is to edge a hard seat with an old rubber car tyre.

Some gardens have tree houses in them, this is fine as long as you are careful. Teach children to climb trees safely, a bad fall can paralyse for life. We must teach children to be careful when they are in a tree house. A little boy died when his tree house caught fire. He had left a candle alight while he slept.

If a refrigerator with an old-type door catch is discarded and left outside, even if only temporarily, make sure the door is removed, or that the catch is smashed. This will prevent children from being trapped. The same precautions should be taken with the newer refrigerators which have magnetic locks, instead of catches, for closing the main door. It is just possible that a small child would be unable to push open this type of door if trapped inside.

If you want to add attractive features, such as waterfalls or fountains, to your garden, or you wish to illuminate these features, contact a specialist. Fitting pumps for fountains and waterfalls is a job for qualified professionals. Garden lamps, pumps for waterfalls and fountains, and floodlights, all need to be waterproof, so unless you are a competent electrician do not attempt this work.

When people decide to have a barbecue party, it often rains on the day, so they move the barbecue indoors, to an extension or the garage maybe. What gets overlooked in the party atmosphere is that any appliance or fuel which needs air for proper combustion must have adequate ventilation to replace the oxygen used up in the air, as well as ventilation to take the fumes away. If sufficient ventilation is lacking, the carbon monoxide produced can build up to a dangerous level and could prove lethal.

DO IT YOURSELF

Many people are doing 'do-it-yourself' these days, because of the recreational satisfaction it brings, and the financial saving! DIY is safe as long as we go about it the correct way and take all possible safety precautions. Knives, scissors, razor blades, glass, power tools and hand tools all take their toll unless we are on our guard and use them wisely.

In Britain, 21 million people require first aid in the home each year as the result of cuts around the home or do-it-yourself activities. Remember, DIY covers everything from putting a nail in a wall to redecorating the wall; anything, even the maintenance of your car, whether you are working in the home, in a shed or workshop, or in the garden or garage.

Think carefully before embarking on any DIY work, and know what you want to do and how to achieve it. There are many excellent books and magazines covering all aspects of DIY, and if you read these you will gain a great deal of valuable information on a variety of subjects, and this will enable you to carry out the work successfully.

Many of the general precautions for DIY are covered in the other chapters. For instance, power tools for drilling, sawing, grinding and sanding are used widely today to take the hard work out of DIY jobs, and the chapter on *Electrical Safety* covers many important points.

DIY also covers cleaning windows or painting the exterior of the house, and the safe use of ladders and step ladders has also been covered. But accidents can happen during seemingly simple operations such as driving a nail in a wall—and the careless use of hammers comes high on the list of accidents. Hand saws and circular saws also cause many problems and great care and concentration must be used when operating such tools. It never pays to be hasty. Never remove guards, and always switch off before putting down a power tool or making adjustments or clearing blockages.

Sharp tools are safer than blunt ones when used correctly, but all tools must be kept away from children. The regular maintenance of all tools is vital to safety.

Eye protection, in the form of goggles or special safety spectacles, should be used for certain jobs: chiselling masonry, operating high speed saws and using some paints and chemicals. Gloves are a wise precaution, particularly when working with glass.

We need to be careful when using glues, especially the instant setting ones as these stick instantly on contact with the skin. If skin does get

Take all possible safety precautions when doing 'do-it-yourself'. Eye protection such as goggles or special safety spectacles is essential when chiselling masonry, operating high-speed saws and using some paints and chemicals. Gloves should be worn when working with glass.

This is dangerous! Never get under a car until the car is supported securely (in this illustration the door could slam and might dislodge the jack). Once jacked up—use safety blocks or ramps as an additional precaution to ensure the vehicle cannot fall on you.

stuck together, do not let the victim rub their eyes or try to pull their fingers apart. Unstick by immersing and washing thoroughly in warm soapy water—get medical advice—and take the victim to the doctor or hospital if necessary.

All DIY chemicals, liquids and products must be kept out of the reach of children. Keep glues well locked away, this avoids accidents and prevents glue-sniffing which is addictive and extremely dangerous.

More and more car maintenance is being carried out at home and there are two major warnings that must be included here. Never crawl or lie under a car until you are quite sure it is jacked up securely, and never leave the engine running in the garage. If an engine test is necessary, carry it out in the open where the exhaust fumes will be diluted and dispersed without harming you or anyone else.

People are taking on far more sophisticated DIY jobs than they were a few years ago and carrying out the work extremely well. But do read instructions and observe all the safety rules, that way you will live to appreciate the good results.

7

HOME IS HOME—EVEN ON HOLIDAY

AWAY FROM IT ALL

When we go on holiday we think we are safe, but many tragic accidents occur because this is the very time we least expect them to happen. Home is home—even on holiday. Whether at a hotel or a boarding house, a rented home or a flat, in a boat, caravan or a tent—when on holiday, where you live becomes your home and the countryside becomes your garden. Be on guard against the unexpected dangers and new hazards which can arise.

The first thing to do is to protect the home you are leaving by switching off and unplugging all electrical appliances and turning off the electricity and gas at the mains. Run down your stock of food in the freezer, if you have one, otherwise you will need to leave the electricity on.

PROTECTING CHILDREN

When you arrive at your destination check on high-chairs and cots before you use them. There can be hazards through bad design, particularly when holidaying abroad. In one case a child slipped through a gap at the base of a cot and was strangled as its body hung there.

Often the sides of cots are not high enough, or the safety catches are faulty, or the bars are not close enough together to prevent babies from pushing their heads through. The mattress may not be thick enough to avoid gaps at the base. Pillows may be soft, if so, do not use them, otherwise an infant might be suffocated. If the pillow is safe, insert it *under* the head of the mattress to provide a slight incline, this way you will be doubly safe. Check that high-chairs and harnesses are safe, and that the door and window catches to balconies are secure.

Dogs have been known to run out of rooms and fall to their death from balconies. Try to guard against unexpected accidents and do take care, accidents happen, even on holiday.

Home is home—even on holiday. Check cots, prams and high-chairs for safety—and read the fire notice so you know exactly what to do in an emergency.

IN THE EVENT OF FIRE

Every day there are fires at hotels and boarding houses. Some are small, others result in injury or death. The causes are many but one which can be avoided occurs through people smoking in bed. Never do this. It puts everyone's lives at risk and it is so easy to drop off to sleep. When smoking at other times always use ashtrays, not waste-paper, refuse or other bins, and always make sure cigarettes are stubbed out and extinguished thoroughly.

One of the first things you should do when you arrive at a hotel or boarding house is read the fire notices. These will tell you what to do in the event of fire, the escape route you should use and everything else you need to know, including how to raise the alarm if you discover a fire. Most fires are discovered between 2300 hours and 0700 hours when people are normally asleep. Read the instructions beforehand; the middle of a fire, in the small hours, when you are bemused, in unfamiliar surroundings and alarmed, is certainly not the best time to do so.

If there is a fire, the important thing is to stay calm and not waste precious time in dressing or in rescuing valuables. Go to the safe assembly point outside, and stay out. Do not attempt to use lifts, the power supply could be interrupted and you could be trapped. Remember to open your door gently and slowly and, as you do so, to stand back against the wall out of the way of blast or flames. If the smoke or the heat outside prevents you from using your escape route or leaving your room, close the door and follow the advice given in the subchapter WHAT TO DO IF TRAPPED BY FIRE. This gives advice on how to prevent smoke from entering the room, how to attract attention from the window while keeping low beside it, and what you should do to ensure survival until the fire brigade arrives to rescue you.

Fires occur on holiday not only in buildings—but also in tents, particularly as it is difficult to make them both flameproof and waterproof at the same time. Caravans and boats also present dangers, with the fires spreading with frightening speed.

Liquid petroleum gas (L.P.G.) is used widely on boats and in tents and caravans and is quite safe if used according to the instructions. Adequate ventilation is essential when using any L.P.G. appliance. A firm level site free from combustible materials must always be chosen. Empty gas cartridges must never be left lying around, nor placed near any source of heat. When you are moving from one location to another, disconnect the gas cylinder from the appliances. Keep the cylinder valve closed at all times when not in use.

Make sure that when a low flame is being used it cannot be extinguished by sudden draughts. If the flame does go out, turn off the gas supply without attempting to relight it. Turn off the cylinder and the

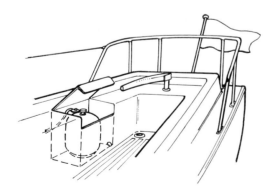

Liquid petroleum gas is a safe, convenient fuel if used according to the instructions. The safety rules given on page 23 must always be observed.

Keep away from low-level areas when camping, as freak rainstorms can cause flooding—and drowning. Never let unattended children play near rivers, lakes, canals, ponds, gravel pits or the sea.

appliance then increase the ventilation to get rid of any gas. When you are sure that all trace of gas has been removed, turn on the supply at the cylinder, and the appliance—and relight the appliance.

If a leak is suspected, turn off the supply and extinguish all flames and naked lights. Do not smoke and thoroughly ventilate the area. A draught should be introduced in boats and caravans—bearing in mind that the gas is heavier than air—to remove all traces of gas from beneath floor boards and at low levels. Engines, electric appliances and switches should never be turned on, run or started up until the craft or caravan is clear of all fumes, otherwise the sparks might cause an explosion.

WATER, WATER EVERYWHERE

Campers should be careful about lighting fires, and should avoid siting tents beside rivers or in low level areas where freak rainstorms might cause rapid flooding and sudden and unexpected drowning.

Risks of drowning arise during other holiday activities. Sea, rivers, lakes, canals, ponds and gravel pits can all prove dangerous, with lives being lost through the disregard of warning notices and normal safety precautions. Watch out for the safety of yourself and your children.

Water from streams should not be used for drinking, as it is almost certain to be polluted these days.

WATCH OUT FOR SHOCKS

Attractive camping sites are not always safe ones. When we find a site we should have a good look round. If a mains electricity supply line runs overhead we should keep well clear. Unforeseen incidents have happened on approved caravan sites. In one instance, a father sent his son out to put up the caravan television aerial. The aerial came into contact with

Avoid electric shocks by siting caravans away from overhead power supplies. Have the electric wiring of the caravan checked regularly. The illustration gives two of the ways that children have been killed while on holiday.

an overhead line carrying 11,000 volts and the boy was killed. This incident is not as remote as it may seem. TV aerials are becoming very sophisticated and some extend to quite a height. Some caravans even have sundecks on their roofs from which people could easily reach up and touch the electric lines.

We need to be sure there are no overhead wires nearby when moving a boat. There have been some bad incidents with sailing boats. Where electricity is concerned, aluminium masts present a danger and so do wooden ones which usually have steel guide wires anchored to the outer perimeter of the boat. The danger from electricity is increased because masts, boats, grass and slipways are usually wet. Whether aluminium or wood, the discharge can come down through someone's body. Alternatively, two overhead electricity lines could short if touched by a mast. So the clear warning is that we should make sure there are no overhead wires before erecting the mast. Never push a boat in the garden, or down to the water, with the mast up and hope it will clear an overhead line.

The electrical wiring and installations of your caravan should have a regular check. This may sound like just another 'do this—do that' warning, but it is based on common-sense and to ignore it is to invite tragedy.

On one occasion a child crawled under a caravan to retrieve a ball. He touched the underneath of the chassis, it was 'live', and he was killed. The supply connection to the caravan was sound, but the wiring of the vehicle was faulty.

8

CHILDREN AT RISK

It is hard to think of anything more tragic, or unnecessary, than for a child to die from choking and suffocation; and yet this is the biggest killer of young children. Burns and scalds, poisoning from medicines or household fluids and products, they all cause fatalities or needless suffering, long-term damage or permanent disfigurement. Although this chapter is mainly concerned with the causes and prevention of accidents to children—remember that adults can fall victim to many of the accidents mentioned. Accidents happen whether you live in North America, South Africa, Australasia or Europe. Over 30,000 accidental deaths occur in the E.E.C. countries each year, with between 4 and 5 million people being injured. This shows the size of the problem.

CHOKING AND SUFFOCATION

This can happen to anyone of any age—but the main victims are babies and children. We have four minutes in which to save a life if someone starts choking or cannot breathe. It is easier to save a life by not allowing the accident to happen.

Choking occurs when the windpipe becomes blocked while eating, or some object is swallowed by mistake, or vomit goes down the wrong way cutting off the supply of air to the lungs—which can lead to a stage where breathing is stopped.

The precautions are simple, but all too often they are overlooked or forgotten. Babies must never be left alone with a bottle to feed themselves. They cannot control the flow of milk and can easily choke. After you have fed a baby, whether from bottle or breast, make sure the baby has got rid of all its 'wind'. If you do not, it can cause danger after you have put the baby in its pram or cot and left the room.

Babies can choke on the sponges used for wiping their mouths after feeding, or washing their faces when bathing. Use a large sponge as a child is less likely to put this in its mouth. Dummies can kill—so always

Children chew almost anything and so cut their mouths on objects with sharp edges. They also swallow almost anything, so give big toys to small children. Teddy bears should have safe fillings and eyes that cannot be pulled out.

buy an approved type that is designed to prevent it from interfering with breathing or being swallowed.

When feeding young children, always be sure to cut the food in small enough pieces before giving it to them.

Rattles, buttons and other small 'foreign' objects, including pins and coins, are frequently picked up by young children and then put in their mouths. These sort of objects should be removed from cots, beds and wherever children play. Care must be taken when buying toys to make sure that the toys, or bits of the toys, will not be put in the mouth and swallowed. For example, a toy that breaks down into several sweet-size pieces is obviously not suitable for young children.

Many things can cause children to suffocate. Rubber or plastic bibs must be removed immediately after feeding. Although there have been many warnings about the danger from the plastic bags so commonly used in our homes today, many children are still being suffocated. Never let them play with plastic bags. Keep all bags, including pedal bin and dustbin liners, stored safely out of reach.

When you dispose of empty plastic bags always tear them or punch holes in them. Children like to play with plastic and if you have forgotten to punch the holes, the plastic can cling to a child's face, blocking the mouth and nose and cutting off the air supply. Destroy the plastic bags after you have brought clothes back from the dry cleaners, and do not use plastic sheets on pillow cases or mattresses.

Pillows in cots have smothered and suffocated many babies—and

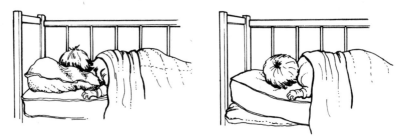

Never use a pillow for a baby under 12 months as the baby could smother and suffocate. Pillows for older babies and young children should be put *under* the mattress.

pillows should never be used for babies under one year. Even some of the so-called 'safety' pillows have proved fatal. If you want to use a pillow for young children in cots or prams, use a porous pillow, as feather filled pillows and some coverings can suffocate. Put the pillow *under* the mattress, that way children are unable to bury their faces in it and suffocate. Never take a baby to bed with you, there have been many cases of accidental smothering.

ACCIDENTAL POISONING FROM MEDICINES
Hospitals the world over are full of children suspected of poisoning themselves, but it is the adults who are to blame, not the children. Adults also poison themselves, through taking accidental overdoses of medicines or through misusing household chemicals and products. In Britain 16,000 children are taken to hospital with suspected poisoning, another 10,000 are treated at home and over 600 people die from accidental poisoning each year. Yet care and forethought on the part of producers and users alike could prevent these accidents.

The most serious dangers come from the swallowing of medicines and household chemicals and fluids left around the house. The one thing everyone should do is keep medicines in a locked cupboard (ideally, in an approved lockable medicine cabinet with child-proof locks). Never imagine it is safe to leave medicines lying around just because they are out of the normal reach of children. This applies to medicines bought over the counter as well as those prescribed by the doctor.

Brightly coloured tablets look like sweets to children, so never take tablets in front of children, they might think you are eating sweets. Never remove medicines from their original containers and put them into other bottles or containers. You might forget which kind of medicine they are.

It is estimated that there are well over a billion (1,000,000,000,000)

94

unwanted tablets in homes in England and Wales at any one time. Old and unused medicines must never be put in the dustbin or the fire. They should be flushed down the lavatory or, safest of all, returned to the chemist where the pharmacist has the facilities, knowledge and means of destroying and disposing of them for you.

When a doctor has prescribed medicine for your children, or yourself, always read the instructions carefully and be sure to give, or take, the exact recommended dose and stick to the correct interval between doses. Never give a medicine prescribed for one person to another person who appears to have a similar ailment as they might have a different ailment and the wrong medicine could prove fatal.

POISONING FROM HOUSEHOLD CHEMICALS AND CLEANERS

A whole new range of dangers have been introduced into our homes with the various chemicals, liquids and household products we use. Bleaches, turpentine and turpentine substitute, paraffin, ammonia, paint solvents, oven cleaners and various other cleansing agents and disinfectants; a lack of respect and care in their use and safe storage can cause poisoning. With children particularly at risk.

In most instances of poisoning the substances were stored within easy reach of children, under the kitchen sink or around the home. Which should be a clear enough warning for us not to do this. All household

Keep household chemicals and cleaners out of the reach of children. This helps avoid accidental poisoning.

Medicines should be kept in child-proof lockable cabinets, preferably with a sloping top to prevent items from being left out accidentally.

Do not overlook Aspirin, sleeping tablets or cosmetics. These are often kept in a bedroom and can be a hazard.

chemicals must be treated with respect. Keep them in their own containers, in a high cupboard if possible, preferably locked and with the key removed, and never leave them unattended during use when there are children about. Lavatory cleaners should not be left on the floor beside the lavatory, an unguarded plastic bottle is a temptation to a child.

Many accidents have been caused by people decanting chemicals into other containers without taking the precaution of clearly labelling them. This puts children at risk, and also concerns adults. People have died because of poisonous liquids consumed from soft drink bottles.

Lead is a cumulative poison which can cause mental retardation and death. Although it is no longer permitted in paints and toys in many countries, it is still something we need to be on our guard against. Some countries still allow its use, and certain products sometimes slip through the import net. Cosmetics should be kept away from children, as children like to dip their fingers in and lick them. A little girl in Birmingham suffered from lead poisoning caused by her mother's hair preparation.

Do not leave alcohol where children can reach it and drink it, it can be a poison.

CARBON MONOXIDE AND GAS POISONING

Proper ventilation is vital when using any gas or oil appliance, and when using open fires, as they require fresh air so that combustion can take place safely and efficiently. We also need fresh air, if there is not sufficient ventilation, or if the gas or other fuel is not burning properly, carbon monoxide poisoning can occur, and can prove fatal, or death may come from asphyxiation due to the exhaustion of the oxygen. Modern insulated homes can present hazards, so can old ones, if they have blocked ventilators and chimneys or damaged flues. When the weather is cold people often block up ventilators. This is unwise as proper venting to the outside of a house is essential at all times of the year.

Small rooms, such as bedrooms and bathrooms, can cause problems. We should make a point of having all appliances, ventilators, flues and chimneys checked regularly. Gas and oil installations and appliances should also be regularly checked and serviced for safety and efficiency. That way you can protect yourself, your family and your neighbours.

Adequate ventilation, and ensuring that ventilators are not blocked, applies (in addition to oil appliances and open fires) to all forms of gas, whether North Sea gas, or town gas (sometimes referred to as manufactured gas), or liquid petroleum gas (L.P.G.).

The bathroom is often forgotten when it comes to safety. If you have a gas water heater make sure it is well ventilated and that the flue system is not broken or damaged. It is best to have installed what is known as a 'balanced flue' sealed gas heater. Open bathroom window or door while drawing off hot water, turn off the gas *before* you get into the bath and do not run more hot water while you are in the bath. Be sure to have the water heater serviced regularly, once a year.

Other general precautions have been covered in the *Fire* chapter, in the sections on gas safety and L.P.G. safety, including what to do if gas leaks are suspected.

Carbon monoxide poisoning can happen in other ways; from car exhaust fumes, for instance. That is why we must never leave the car engine running when the car is in the garage.

Garages must be sealed off if attached to a house.

BURNS AND SCALDS

Anyone who has visited the burns unit of a specialised hospital is unlikely to forget the experience. 80% of the victims (of all age groups) are there because of accidents in the home. Burns and scalds are not only frightening and extremely painful, they are also the cause of severe psychological disturbance. Burns often need plastic surgery and skin grafting that can take months or years, and sometimes they disfigure for life. And yet, like most accidents, they can be avoided.

The kitchen and bathroom are the most obvious danger areas. It is an essential precaution that young children are not allowed to race

Tablecloths should not be used when there are young children about. Children pull on tablecloths, and thousands of children end up burnt, scalded or injured each year.

around in the kitchen when food is being cooked. Sometimes it is impossible to keep them out, they need the table for homework, or they are
too young to be left alone. In which case burns and scalds can be avoided
if you fit a cooker guard to make it more difficult for children to reach
up and tip over the pans.

If you are not using a guard—turn the pan handles away from the
front of the cooker, but watch out for your own safety. Never position
the handles over a heat source, or you might end up as the casualty, with
bad burns on your hands. A cloth or an oven glove is a must when using
a cooker—and it pays to wear close-fitting flame-resistant or low flamm-
ability clothing. Toys should be kept out of the kitchen. You might trip,
fall and burn yourself or sustain some other injury.

Scalds can be extremely serious, so be careful with the electric kettle
and keep its flex away from children. Never pour while the kettle is
switched on, and never rush pouring, whatever the type of kettle. Steam
can scald, so can hot fat, tea, coffee and any other hot fluid. This is
the reason why the edges of tablecloths should be turned under, that way
children will not pull at the edges and bring hot liquids or foods tumbling
down on to them. In fact, it is worth doing without a tablecloth when
children are young.

The bath is also dangerous, used wrongly it can kill. Always put the
cold water in first, then add the hot water. This is for the safety of children
and the elderly. Always test the temperature with a thermometer or your
elbow before putting a baby in the bath, also do this when washing them
at a basin. Never leave children in a bath unattended, and never fill a
bath too full, many children have been drowned.

When you use a hot-water-bottle check that it is not too hot, always
use a thick cover on it and remove the bottle before you put the
child to bed. At the end of a day, when you are tired, it is easy to let
your concentration slip. If a child or anyone wants a hot drink, make
sure it is not too hot. Burns or scalds of the mouth or throat can be painful
and serious. And remember, burns can also be caused by corrosive

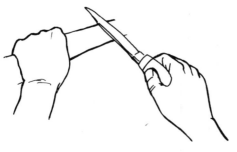

Cuts account for a third of
all home accidents. When
you use a knife—any
knife—be sure to cut *away*
from yourself.

Injuries arise and complications can set in when pieces of broken glass, pottery or porcelain are picked up by hand. Always use a dustpan and brush.

liquids, so extreme care is required when using these.

Severe burns or scalds of any type must receive prompt hospital treatment. What you should do in the case of an accident is covered in the chapter on *First Aid* (pp 148–149).

CUTS

Almost all of us have cut ourselves at some time or another, so it is not surprising that cuts account for a third of all accidents in and around the home. Every year there are many very serious accidents, and some fatal (these are mentioned in the chapter on *Glass*). The majority are non-fatal, though still often serious—and they usually result from care-lessness.

One common cause of an accident is through leaving household and garden tools, and other sharp items lying around, and through using them incorrectly. When sharp knives are required they should always be used *away* from you—and not towards the other hand holding the object being cut. When tin-openers are used do not prise the can lids open with your fingers.

Sharp knives, razor blades, scissors, pins and needles must be kept in a safe place away from children.

Whenever glass, pottery or porcelain are broken, do not attempt to pick up the pieces with your fingers as this is how many injuries happen. Sweep up the pieces and wrap them in thick newspaper or place them in a tin and wrap it in several layers of paper. Secure the 'parcel' with string or sticky tape so that the contents cannot spill out. Having swept the floor, use a vacuum cleaner to pick up any tiny slivers or splinters that have been missed or are not visible.

Many dressing-tables, chests, occasional tables and coffee tables have glass tops on them. Sometimes these are not fixed but rely on their own weight to keep them in place. Unfortunately a layer of air frequently gets under the glass so that it slides on a floatation of air, rather like a hover-craft, with the corners being misaligned and slightly jutting. Accidents can occur when people move about in the vicinity, unless the glass tops are permanently secured. The metal edges of kitchen cupboards can cause severe cuts, and cupboard doors should never be left open.

Another problem can be caused by wall-mounted porch lights placed just outside the front door. These are often of a wrought-iron design with a sharp point reaching down from the base. Heads get gashed, particularly those of children being carried and visitors who do not know the house very well. So avoid purchasing any lamp that could be dangerous. If you already have one installed and do not want to part with it, press a cork into the offending point, paint the cork to match the lamp and the problem will be solved.

TOYS AND RECREATIONAL HAZARDS
Although some countries apply strict regulations governing the manu-facture and sale of *safe* toys, children still get hurt, cut, grazed, suffo-cated and choked, so we need to be on our guard when buying toys for children.

One main problem facing toy manufacturers is that children will chew or swallow almost anything.

It is a good idea to give big toys to small children. Small things like beads, soldiers or marbles can be put in the mouth, nose or ear. If you are planning to give a child a teddy bear, check that the filling is safe and that the eyes cannot be pulled out. Avoid purchasing toys that have sharp edges, corners or points; and, although it seems obvious, never give them anything made from glass or china.

Balloons seem safe enough, but teach children how to use them. Many suck in instead of blowing out and end up with the balloon lodged in their windpipe. Pencils and paint brushes get put in the mouth, and if a child falls or bumps into something—one can imagine the consequences. Remember that safe toys can become unsafe if misused—and that all toys can be dangerous if left lying around where they can cause people to fall. Always store toys away when they are not in use.

Parents often cause unexpected hazards when trying to be kind. To give just one example, the lampshades on the ceilings of some bedrooms look like the opened canopy of a parachute. Parents have been known to complete the illusion by adding strings for shroud lines and hanging a small doll from the strings. The problem is that a child will invariably want to reach up and touch the hanging doll, this might lead to a fall. Alternatively, the child might reach the toy in safety, but want to tug at it or make it swing. Or the wind coming through a door or window might make it swing. In either case the electric flex is likely to become damaged and this could cause an electrical short or start a fire.

Young children are excited when given presents, especially at Christmas time, and they should be shown how to use their new toys in safety. Fashions change in toys, and it would be a dull old world if they did not, but as new ones are introduced, some of them inevitably produce hazards. Skateboarding was extremely popular in America for a number of years before it was introduced into Britain. And, after a number of accidents, it was gradually realised that, like many other sports, it required a certain amount of skill, commonsense and protective clothing.

While it was a craze skateboarding gave immense pleasure to masses of children and it was a sport that everyone could take part in. But accidents occurred through loss of balance, boards slipping from under users, collisions and dozens of other reasons. The use of gloves, pads, helmets, chin-straps and other protective equipment could have prevented many of these accidents, but just because there have been accidents we should not think of banning a sport, we should consider how to make it safe. A world which restricted sport because of the dangers would be intolerable.

So with any new toy or sport, it is up to the parents to learn all they can about the particular subject or product and educate their children in its safe and sensible use.

It is also up to us to see that children never play with dangerous objects which are not intended as toys. Children must not be allowed to hide in cupboards, cases or the boots of motor-cars.

NEVER LEAVE CHILDREN ON THEIR OWN
In some countries parents can be prosecuted for neglect if children come to harm when left alone or if the children are repeatedly left alone.

Children left alone, even teenagers, have been killed or badly injured in fires or when falling downstairs. They have been electrocuted, poisoned, suffocated, drowned and have suffered from every other type of accident one can think of. Many mothers are out at work when children come home from school, this can often lead to hazards while playing, doing homework or cooking.

If you do have to go out and leave a baby-sitter make sure they know what to do and how children should be looked after. Give them an address or telephone number where they can reach you in an emergency, and give them the number of the doctor, and make sure they know how to call the fire brigade, ambulance and police. Warn them to check regularly on the children, particularly if the children are in bed, and not to think that their presence is enough.

Warn them that while they read or watch television, children could be at risk, or need help urgently and be too afraid or shy to ask for it— or unable to shout.

9

HYGIENE IN THE HOME

Hygiene in the home is more than just a question of being house-proud, it is vital to the health and general well-being of everyone in the house. Covering everything from general household and personal cleanliness to the correct handling and preparation of foods, the need for clean and antiseptic drains and dustbins—and a sensible approach to the keeping and care of pets.

FOOD POISONING
Millions of people suffer from food poisoning each year, even in the most advanced and sophisticated countries. In some cases the poisoning causes little discomfort, in others it can involve prolonged suffering which leads to death.

Clean kitchens are essential, but not everyone has 'dream kitchens' or easy to clean walls, floors and work-surfaces. Yet even the older types of kitchen can be kept safe by regular cleaning with hot water and a good disinfectant. In any case, whether the kitchen is an old or new one, the utensils and surfaces used during the preparation of food and drinks must always be cleaned thoroughly before and after use and wiped dry with a clean cloth.

It usually comes as a surprise to learn that masses of germs live and grow on our skin. Some of these micro-organisms are good and serve as a protection for our skin, others can be harmful. If the skin is damaged, the germs can set up an infection and anyone who handles food with a cut or sores is a potential danger to others, with the germs being spread about the kitchen, into the food being prepared, and on all the utensils. *Staphylococcal* poisoning arises when food is prepared by someone suffering from a skin, nose or throat infection—and it affects cold meats, pies and milky foods in particular. If it is not possible for anyone to take your place in the kitchen, you will need to be extra careful about cleanliness. Be sure to wash your hands thoroughly, and cover the damaged or infected areas of your skin with a good waterproof dressing. If you can, avoid sneezing or coughing when preparing and handling food.

Salmonella is another type of poisoning to guard against. One of the problems is that contaminated food can look and taste normal. Salmonella generally occurs when food is either kept too long, or is used when warm and not thoroughly heated or cooked. Salmonella germs can be present when you bring food into the kitchen straight from the shops. They are often present in prepared meats and pies, bread and cakes, cream and ice cream, uncooked eggs and poultry. Food can also become contaminated by vermin, by flies and by us. But the one thing salmonella does not like is heat.

Many of the dangers can be avoided by re-heating previously cooked food such as stews to boiling point for a few minutes. This will kill any germs. Cooked foods, which you need to store, should be put into the refrigerator straight away—but although this slows down the growth of the germs, the food must be brought to the boil before using it. Frozen meats, and poultry in particular, must always be thawed before cooking—and must then be heated long enough to destroy the micro-organisms lurking in the centre. Another precaution is to think twice before you eat a raw egg. You will be far safer if you cook it. Any food suspected of being contaminated or in poor condition should never be used, nor fed to animals who can also suffer food poisoning.

USING A DEEP FREEZE

Most homes have refrigerators—and an increasing number are making use of the many advantages to be gained from freezers and fridge freezers. All food must be in perfect condition and must be handled as little as possible. It should be frozen as soon as possible after gathering or preparation. If some simple rules are followed the food will retain its original taste and quality, and it will be impossible to tell that the food was frozen.

Vegetables should always be blanched in boiling water to retard the action of a natural chemical substance called an enzyme. Otherwise the enzymes can spoil the colour and flavour. Food is also spoilt by the natural activity of many different micro-organisms, including moulds, yeasts and bacteria.

The chemical agents of enzymes bring about the ripening of fruit and vegetables. They also ensure the good flavour and tenderness of meat hung for the correct period. But beyond a certain stage—the enzyme activity leads to a rapid deterioration in the food.

Moulds thrive in moist conditions and in hot, humid weather. *Yeasts* are used in cooking—but certain types also attack foods. *Bacteria* can be extremely harmful because they multiply rapidly and they are often the main cause of gastro-enteritis and food poisoning. The faster food is frozen, the sooner any spoilage is slowed to a minimum.

Most micro-organisms are inactive once the food reaches − 10°centigrade, while enzymes function so slowly at the recommended freezer temperature of − 18° centigrade that food has a high quality storage life (determined by the various storage times recommended for each type of frozen food). Food eaten within the correct time presents no health hazard.

Freezers can only preserve food in the state in which it is frozen. Poor quality food will not be improved by freezing, and health-safety can only come from the correct freezing, cooking, storage and thawing, and strict attention to cleanliness and high standards of hygiene.

If mishandling prior to freezing has allowed large numbers of micro-organisms to grow and produce toxins, freezing will not rectify this dangerous situation. It is therefore essential to select high quality fresh produce for freezing, and to prepare it in clean hygienic conditions. Hands and utensils must be clean, and the kitchen must be clear of flies and anything else that can contaminate the food.

It is vital to follow the recommended thawing methods and times. All foods contain a certain amount of water which forms ice crystals during the freezing process. Considerable heat has to be absorbed to change the ice into water. If foods such as meat and poultry are inadequately thawed before cooking, a layer of ice may still surround some micro-organisms and cooking may fail to destroy them.

Freezing is the simplest way of preserving food. It is also a very safe method, provided that sufficient care is taken.

THE RIGHT TAP

Many people fill kettles from the hot tap, but they would not if they looked at the inside of their supply tank in the attic. Even when covered with a lid the contents of the supply tank can have dirt in them. This can include dead mice and birds. As people in a hurry to make a cup of coffee or tea sometimes pour the water without letting it quite boil, the germs do not get killed. The safe way is to draw kettle water and drinking water from the cold tap which brings fresh water straight from the mains supply. This water will also contain oxygen which will make the drink taste better.

THE WEAK LINK

Flies and wasps are a constant health hazard, they carry all kinds of germs and they should be discouraged in every way. Waste food and scraps should be wrapped before being put in the dustbin and dustbins should be kept clean. So should the drains in and around the home. Otherwise they provide the weak link in your hygiene standards.

PET HYGIENE

Many homes have dogs, cats or other pets—but doctors are becoming increasingly concerned about the lack of awareness people show regarding the dangers from diseases transferred by pets.

These include asthma and lung complaints, nervous disorders, multiple sclerosis (linked to canine distemper), epilepsy, liver disease and various kinds of allergies and skin infections, and one of the most alarming diseases, toxocariasis, which leads to blindness or the loss of an eye from an infection passed on by tiny eggs from dogs fouling homes, gardens, pavements and parks. This affects children in particular.

The list is frightening, but it does not mean you must get rid of the pets in your home. You might just as well decide not to live in a house because they can be dangerous. Pets give a tremendous amount of pleasure, all you have to do is observe some clear-cut health and hygiene safety rules. See the pets are inoculated and wormed regularly, and are given a yearly check-up by a veterinary surgeon.

Do not allow pets to lie on beds, pillows or cushions, or climb on chairs and settees. Never let them eat or drink from the same dishes as you. Do not allow anyone to kiss an animal or let an animal lick people. And do not allow a pet, such as a budgerigar, to take food from a person's mouth. If an animal is not yet house trained, do not let anyone come into contact with its excrement, this particularly applies to babies who crawl around on all fours. A thorough cleaning job should be carried out, using detergent and hot water, followed by a wipe over with a suitable disinfectant. Make sure hands are washed after contact with pets, whenever food or drinks are being prepared, and also before all meals.

The cages of birds such as budgerigars and parrots must be cleaned and maintained hygienically, and if they become sick, consult a veterinary surgeon. Exotic pets should never be cuddled and kissed, and hands must be washed after any contact with them.

Some countries have legislation which forbids or restricts the keeping as pets of certain mammals, birds and reptiles. In any event, many pets must live outside in cages or in other suitable shelters—these include rabbits, guinea-pigs, mice, rats, ferrets and tortoises. Never keep any of these inside the home, no matter how much children plead for the pets to be allowed to do so.

10

THE ELDERLY, PEOPLE LIVING ALONE
AND THE DISABLED

It is sad that people complain about growing old when one considers the numbers who die before their time and are denied the privilege. The aim of this book is to help prevent people of all ages from being killed or injured in accidents in the home. And although much of the advice given in each chapter applies to young and old alike— additional safeguards are necessary for the elderly, for those who live alone and for the disabled, all of whom have special problems and hazards to overcome.

Everyone accepts that when a piece of machinery gets old its performance tends to drop off, and it must be treated and used more carefully. Yet this is often overlooked when people grow old. Some men and women live to be ninety or a hundred and manage to remain active, but the majority of people slow down and find it difficult to move about or complete chores in the home or garden. They grow tired more easily, and experience a gradual lessening of their five senses with the passing of the years.

Although this ageing process is quite normal, it can put elderly people at risk as they are less alert and less able to avoid hazardous situations or act quickly if a dangerous situation does arise. Furthermore, when they do have an accident, such as a fall, it usually takes them much longer to recover from the injuries. Normally, the warning signals of our five senses serve to alert us to danger and prompt us to take the necessary avoiding action. To appreciate dangers it obviously helps if we can see them. Adequate lighting, particularly on stairs and in passageways, helps us avoid one of the greatest hazards—falls. But if our eyesight is not so good, we must take extra care and extra precautions to avoid accidents. Failing eyesight may need glasses for correction, or, if you already have glasses, it may need consultation with an optician to improve the lenses of your existing ones.

Our sense of smell is also vital to our safety. If we cannot smell burning there is a greater risk of our being poisoned by chemical fumes, or being killed or injured when a house and its furnishings catch fire. Our other senses, of taste, touch and hearing, help protect us from danger, and if they become diminished they could lead to a time-lag with our slower reactions putting us in danger. As we approach and reach retirement and old age we need to train ourselves to remain alert, so that we are constantly aware of the additional dangers that old age brings. Elderly people should try to remember to take the extra precautions necessary to avoid accidents. They should remember to turn off the electricity at plugs and appliances, to turn off gas taps when not in use—and to light the burner as soon as they have turned on the gas tap. Points about safety in the home and garden are covered in the other chapters, and it is vital that the elderly, the disabled and people living alone should read those chapters. These additional safety tips are designed to alert you to the sort of things which can be overlooked—yet which can make all the difference to the leading of a happier and more active life.

It is wise for the elderly to be more deliberate in their movements. They should get in and out of their chairs slowly but positively, and should avoid making sudden turns or impulsive movements as these can cause dizziness and lead to a fall. The design of an armchair is important, as it is far easier and safer if you can sit down and get up from a higher chair rather than from a low one.

Slippers are usually more comfortable than shoes, but some types con-

Elderly people should choose their slippers and shoes carefully. The soles should be non-slip. Avoid rushing when getting into and out of chairs and avoid turning suddenly or doing anything which might cause dizziness or result in a fall.

tribute to falls. Avoid rubber or composition-soled slippers and go for leather-soles as these are far safer on the varied floor surfaces of a house. Avoid frills and unnecessary trimmings on slippers and make sure they are kept in good repair. Rubber-soled shoes are safer than slippers when walking on wet paving stones, other hard surfaces or wet grass.

It gets less easy to touch our toes as we get older and, similarly, it becomes more difficult to bend, stoop or stretch. The things you need frequently should be placed where they can be reached easily, without you having to do anything that can cause dizziness or loss of balance. It is impossible to put everything at a convenient level, but you should never attempt to stand on a chair or other item to get something that is out of your reach. Always use household steps and take your time. Some steps have padded seats on the top, but these tops should only be used for sitting on as you could slip or lose your balance if you stand.

Many elderly people fall when walking in the house or garden. There would be fewer accidents if walking sticks were used. Those who are old in limb but young in mind are often reluctant to use sticks as they believe that sticks make them *look* old and draw attention to themselves. However, walking with a stick is far more dignified than falling over without one. The use of a walking stick shows commonsense, even more so, if you take the precaution of using one with a rubber end.

If gardening becomes difficult you may have to ease up on some things. Many elderly people have solved the problems concerned with pruning,

An upturned wooden box or crate can help the elderly to avoid bending and stooping, and so enable them to enjoy their gardening.

weeding and tending of flower borders by sitting on an upturned wooden box so they can work at their own pace without having to stoop.

Accidents in the garden happen more often during the winter months, through falls caused by freezing and slippery conditions. Indoors, the sitting-room is the most frequently used room, and accidents can occur if the elderly are alone there. So guards must be fixed to all heaters, spark-guards being placed round open fires and left there whenever the occupier leaves the room, even if only gone for a few moments. Care must be taken when filling hot-water-bottles. This should be done slowly over the sink, and should never be rushed; and a bottle should not be used in bed without a cover on it.

The misuse of electric blankets and the lack of regular maintenance have led to fires and other accidents involving injury and death. Information on their correct use is contained in the chapter on *Fire,* together with further safety points on all electrical equipment in the chapter on *Electrical Safety.*

There is a scheme which can save lives. British Gas state that if you are elderly, or a handicapped person of any age, and you live alone, you can have a free gas safety check of your installations and appliances which includes minor repairs. Ask your local social services or welfare organisation to arrange this for you. Where costly repairs prove necessary, these organisations or your local gas service may be able to help make arrangements for you. But talk to them *before* you order any costly work.

HYPOTHERMIA – DANGERS FROM LOW TEMPERATURE

One problem facing the elderly and people living alone is knowing how to keep warm. The high cost of fuel causes hardship, and every winter there are reports of people becoming victims of hypothermia, becoming unconscious or dying from extreme cold in inadequately heated homes.

As people get older their bodies begin to lack the ability to regulate temperature. Many victims have died while asleep in cold bedrooms. Others have died when their bedcovers slipped and their body-heat drained away.

Normally when the body loses heat and becomes cold its natural re-action is to increase the heat by muscular activity. This is why we shiver automatically. But this heat cannot last for long. Fat people have a slight advantage as they have more built-in insulation than thin people. But in the case of hypothermia victims, the mental and physical systems gradually run down until the victim becomes unconscious.

Hypothermia can also occur during the daytime, when old people are sitting alone. One of the difficulties of hypothermia is that it is difficult

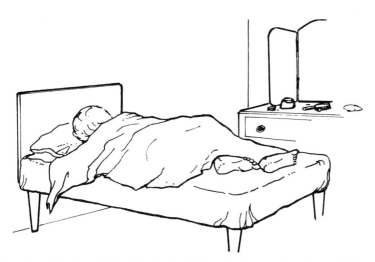

Hypothermia is a hazard facing the elderly and those who live alone in inadequately heated homes. Immediate medical help must be obtained if an elderly person is found unconscious or ill in conditions of extreme cold. See FIRST AID section for symptoms and action to take.

to detect, and it can be mistaken for a 'stroke' or heart attack. If ever you find an old person ill, unconscious or lying immobilised on the floor in a cold house in cold weather, hypothermia should be suspected and medical help should be summoned immediately.

The victim's temperature may be below the lowest scale recorded on a household thermometer. If their temperature is below 35° centigrade (95° fahrenheit) this low temperature is enough to confirm suspicions of hypothermia. Their skin will be very cold to the touch.

If someone is cold, the natural reaction is to warm them but, with hypothermia, rewarming must be slow and gradual—otherwise the sudden change of temperature could kill. Always call immediately for an ambulance and medical help. The correct action to take is given in detail in the *First Aid* chapter under HYPOTHERMIA.

When the victim is admitted to hospital, the doctors will know what to do and will have the knowledge and facilities to gradually warm the victim—a process which may take several days. The victim will be treated for possible infection and other complications.

LIVING ALONE AND KEEPING WARM
People of the past went to bed in nightcaps and bedsocks, and they knew what they were doing. A tremendous amount of heat is lost through the

top of our heads. It is worse for men as they have the added disadvantages of having shorter hair and going bald as they grow older. Considerable heat loss can be lessened if an elderly person wears a warm and safe covering for the top of the head and warm woollen socks—not only in bed but at all times in very cold conditions.

It is better to keep warm during the daytime by wearing several layers of thin clothes, rather than wearing one thick layer. Try to keep the bedroom and the sitting-room warm—but be sure to keep all heating appliances away from the bed and furnishings, and take all the other fire safety precautions. Make sure the bed is covered with sufficient blankets, and make sure they are secure and cannot slip off the bed. It helps if rooms are draughtproof, but do not forget that appliances using flame for heating need ventilation.

Fuel bills are enough to frighten anybody these days. You can economise by closing off any room you are not using, but do keep the others warm. The fuel authorities in Britain, and in some other countries, will not cut off supplies to pensioners in cases of genuine hardship. It may be possible to obtain heating allowances or other grants.

Some people spread the cost of the heating bill by making a regular monthly payment. Others regularly buy savings stamps.

One thing that is often overlooked during cold weather, when people feel 'down', is that food is fuel for our bodies. No matter how we feel, we will feel better and keep warmer if we make sure we eat one good hot meal a day. Cold weather can arrive unexpectedly, and when it comes you will probably not feel like going out to shop, so be prepared and have a supply of food, soups and the ingredients for hot drinks available in the house.

Elderly people living alone usually do not like bothering neighbours. Neighbours, in turn, often do not like to interfere, although they probably want to help and would be pleased to keep an eye on you. Do not be afraid to ask them. Everyone needs help at some time. In any event, if you are really cold and unwell, the one person you must contact is your doctor. If you are cold and remain cold—apart from the danger of hypothermia—you will not be able to think properly or co-ordinate your movements and you might have an accident.

CALLS FOR HELP

About 2 million elderly people live alone in Britain—and countless people die yearly because they are unable to get urgent help when they need it.

A telephone is a vital aid in an emergency, but it is not always the answer because sometimes elderly accident victims cannot reach it and sometimes they are unable to speak. *Alarm systems* are available in many

A call for help has already been made by this victim through the portable control unit in her hand. This is one of many alarm systems available which summon aid, often from several miles away.

countries and can be of great help to the disabled and to people living alone. Alarms can take the form of flashing lights, ringing bells or automatic systems which call for help—sometimes over a distance of several miles. When the elderly need help they need it fast. If an elderly person falls they may be unable to get up. One emergency system consists of a control unit which can be carried and operated from anywhere in the house. The pressing of a button in the case of an emergency bring_ a pre-recorded cassette message into action. A small transmitter (mounted in the home) calls for help, giving precise information about the victim's name and address and the fact that they require immediate help. You can pre-code several telephone numbers—friends, relatives, neighbours, anyone who is willing to help.

The system automatically dials the numbers so that your call is certain to be answered by someone. The system is operated by rechargeable batteries—so it can still operate even if there is a power cut or other electrical failure.

When the call is answered the victim can hear the reply over a loudspeaker, so there is the double comfort in knowing that help is on the way.

There are a number of different alarm systems with new ones being introduced all the time. You can find out about them by contacting the Post Office or other welfare organisations for the disabled or people living alone, in the country you live in.

THE DISABLED AND HANDICAPPED
If you are disabled there are aids to make life easier. There are special telephones to help people who cannot see properly, or who are hard of hearing or who have difficulty with speech or are handicapped and have restricted or limited movement.

Special taps and handles are available, as are controls which can be fitted to cookers, lights and other electrical or gas appliances to make them easier to use. Braille-marked controls are also available.

Sensible seats for use in the bath are available, so that you do not have to lower or raise yourself very far. Aids for when you use the lavatory and aids to help you wash at the basin or take a shower are made, as are special adjustable beds, walking aids, shoes suitable for use with calipers, and self-propelled or electrically operated wheelchairs. There is even a device to help with reading, it will turn over the pages of a book. Maybe you know about this and are using one now.

If you think that any of these, and numerous other aids, can help you, contact your doctor, local authority or the disabled and other welfare organisations for advice. Some countries give financial help in certain circumstances, taking the view that it is better to prevent people from having accidents than to treat them in hospital and waste time and resources in doing so.

AVOIDING MISTAKES WITH MEDICINES

It is very easy for people to make mistakes when taking drugs and medicines. Some drugs make people feel drowsy and this can cause them to repeat a dose, or take a dose when they should not. Apart from the dangers in doing this, if their mental faculties become obscured they will be more prone to accidents.

Precautions must be taken, and one of them is never to take medicines in the dark. If there is medical approval for you taking medicine at night, turn on the bedside lamp before you take the dose. To help you find the light it is wise to have a torch handy. If you need glasses these should be kept by the bedside, and a magnifying glass is also a good idea.

With all medicines, whenever they are to be taken, always read and follow the instructions on the label. Take the exact recommended dose and stick to the interval between doses. If you have to take medicine regularly, a wise precaution is to measure out the daily dose which might consist of several of the same tablets or a mixture of different tablets. Then, if you take the tablets at the right intervals, you will be safe and will not swallow more than the recommended 24 hour supply. Some pills are prescribed 'to be taken as required' with a warning not to exceed more than a certain number each week. The wisest answer is to measure out the week's supply, on a regular day, such as Sunday, and refill to make up the numbers on the same day a week later.

All medicines must be kept in safe clearly marked containers, so that you know what you are taking—and they must be kept out of the reach of children.

11

SAVING YOUR BACK

Millions suffer from back trouble, with the pain being so great that in many cases the victims are unable to work, or shop, or carry out the daily running of a home.

Anyone who has suffered from this trouble will tell you how nasty the pain can be. Everyone has toothache at some time or another. Imagine what it would be like to have acute toothache all over your body, not just in your back but also in your legs, your shoulders, your neck and the front and back of your head. Add the feeling of hot needles being stuck into you and muscles being stretched like an elastic band to breaking point—and you will have an idea of how agonising back pain can be. And that is by no means a complete description. It can be worse—with the complaint causing enforced immobilisation for long periods.

The causes are many and varied, and baffling even to the experts. People often suffer from back pain if they spend their time sitting at an office desk, or driving a vehicle—but most cases occur when people have to lift heavy weights at work. Lifting also has to be done in the home and garden and we can increase our chances of avoiding back pain if we learn to lift things correctly.

LIFTING
It is obviously in everyone's interest to lift things the right way. Not only heavy objects—but also light ones. People have put their backs out when bending over incorrectly to pick up a piece of paper.

Most cases of back pain are caused by spraining or straining a muscle or joint in the spinal column. The bones of this column are separated from each other by discs designed to absorb shock between the vertebrae, the discs also act as bearings when twisting. Back pain can result from a disc moving slightly and pressing on a nerve. When this happens, acute pain can be felt in the back and in the neck, arms and legs.

To avoid temporary, accumulative or irreversible damage to muscles and discs, all objects must be lifted and *moved* correctly. So we should plan in advance what we want to lift, how we are going to carry it, and where we want to put it. If the object is too heavy for us, we should not attempt to lift it without assistance. This may seem obvious but many people insist that they can manage, ignore the warning, then go ahead and ruin their back. Women should be especially careful as they have a lighter skeletal structure and this can produce certain problems.

Most of us have lifted and moved things in the wrong way for years, it is not easy for us to change our habits—but we must.

The first thing we must learn is *never bend over or twist your body* when lifting, pushing or carrying things. Apart from unnatural stresses put on the spinal column and the damage this can cause, doing this virtually removes the mainstay and leaves the spinal column to rely upon muscle support. If the back is kept straight, everything 'locks' into its rightful place, remains that way and gives us stability.

The golden rule when lifting is to keep a straight back and bend from the knees. This lets the leg and thigh muscles take the weight.

You will need to get close to the object, to avoid bending even slightly. Make sure you are well balanced and, if possible, already pointing in the direction in which you wish to move the object. Arms should be held in close to the side of the body, chin tucked in—with the whole of the

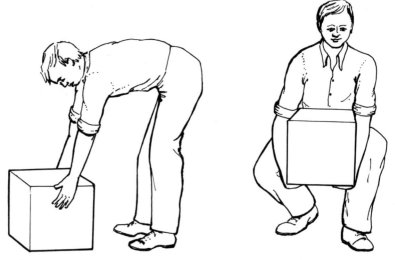

To avoid back injuries avoid bending like this. Always keep a straight back and bend from the knees when lifting objects or putting them down.

Pushing in this way can lead to back injuries.

A straight back, angled at about 55° to the ground, with arms straight out in front, chin tucked in and one foot in advance of the other is the easiest and safest way to push large objects.

fingers right under the object (not just the fingertips). When you have a firm hold, lift with a smooth action (never a jerk), keeping your back straight (never twist it). This allows the powerful leg and thigh muscles to do the lifting.

Keep your back straight as you carry the object. Do not bend, and keep the weight held close to your body. Step carefully, without rushing, and when you come to put the object down, bend the knees to lower the object—never bend your back.

Sacks containing peat, fertiliser or other gardening materials can be a problem to lift. The same rules apply about bending from the knees and keeping a straight back. Having lifted one end of the bag, step forward so that the top end you have just lifted rests against your knees, then lower your body, bending at the knees, and put your fingers under the sack, where the sack touches the ground, and lift correctly.

PUSHING

If you have to push an object, remember to keep your back straight and keep your arms straight in front of you against the object. Keep your chin tucked in. Pushing in this way, with your whole body tilted forward so that your rear leg, your back and the back of your head form a continuous straight line at about 55° to the ground, will keep you from injuring your back.

Golfers are only successful when they use skill, not brute force, to get the best results. The same applies when trying to lift or move things in the house or garden.

12

MOVING HOME

SAFETY CHECKS

A great deal of lifting is involved in moving home, even when the bulk of the work is done by professional removal contractors. The rules about lifting things correctly must be followed if you are to avoid the risk of back injury. Even more than normal care and concentration will be needed, as you will be moving about in unfamiliar surroundings, and will probably be tired. If you can plan ahead so you know what is to go where, you can tell the removal men and it will save you a lot of unnecessary lifting later.

Other safety precautions will be necessary to avoid the hazards contained in the other chapters of this book. Completely new fire drills will be required, owing to the changed locations of the rooms in the new home. These should be practised early on. If you do not have a telephone or if it has not yet been installed, find out where the nearest public call-box is, in case you have to use it in an emergency.

You will need to find out where the electricity mains switches and fuse board are located. You will also need to know the gas mains supply and the position of the water mains stop-cock. You will probably need to arrange for the disconnection and reconnection of some of the following: a cooker, a washing machine, a freezer, night storage heaters. This should be done well in advance—never attempt to do this work yourself.

The previous owners of your new home may not have been safety conscious, and it may be necessary to have electrical wiring and gas safety checks carried out by qualified engineers. Boiler flues and chimneys may need to be swept.

If you have purchased the existing carpets and mats these will require checking, to see that they are firmly secured and cannot lead to falls. Your new house might have larger areas of glass and everyone will need to be on their guard against this. The stairs may require more illumination to make them safe. The bathroom might require work to see that general safety rules are not broken.

Quite often we seriously underestimate the hazards presented by a new house and we must always look at our new home with a critical eye. It will present a set of entirely new circumstances, for children for example. Safety barriers may be needed at the top and bottom of stairs, and windows must be checked to see that they are safe, and that children cannot fall out of them.

Walk around the garden to see if pools are safe or if they need alteration. Check the fastenings on gates to make sure children cannot run into the road. Some of the plants growing in the garden might be poisonous, so check on these too. Trees should be inspected otherwise branches might come tumbling down on people, or on the house itself. Some of the tiles on the roof may be loose—so these will need replacing to avoid accidents. The windows may be higher, or larger or smaller, and so more difficult to clean. Extra care must be taken when using a ladder to reach them.

When you come to mow the lawn, the previous owners may have left stones which could be sent flying with disastrous results. Clear away the stones before cutting the grass.

If there are any open and unfenced areas of grass adjoining your home which belong to your property—you have every right to ask people not to allow their dogs to foul the area.

Many people forget about doctors and dentists when they move to a new area. Register right away—you never know when you or anyone else in your home will need one. Also make a point of finding out the location of your nearest hospital.

FIRST AID

The author wishes to express his most grateful thanks for the kind assistance and time devoted by an area surgeon of the St. John Ambulance Association in helping to compile the first aid sections which follow.

FIRST AID INDEX

FIRST AID SECTION

Whenever first aid is required, it is likely to be needed in a hurry. So you must remain calm—act quickly—and know exactly what you should do. In serious cases you should immediately call for an ambulance. In other cases you should call for a doctor. While you are waiting for professional medical help you will need to give first aid treatment—and for this you will need certain items and supplies close at hand.

FIRST AID KIT
A first aid kit is essential to every home. When needed nothing else will take its place—it may make all the difference between success and disaster by preventing injury or loss of blood from becoming more serious than they need be.

The first aid kit should be clearly labelled. It should be placed on a shelf out of the reach of children—but must be located where everyone in the home knows where it is.

You can purchase first aid kits for the home—these vary in content and price and some tend to be rather expensive—or you can make up your own kit. If you decide to 'do-it-yourself' do not have a lock on the box. In an emergency you could waste precious seconds looking for the key. A plastic box makes the best container as it will probably have an airtight lid and will be rot-proof. It will also be light and convenient to take with you when you go on holiday; or when a caravan, tent or boat becomes your temporary home.

The following items should prove adequate to deal with most emergencies requiring first aid

Gauze dressings
Cotton wool
Continuous strip dressing, 2 in. width (5.08 cm)
Adhesive wound dressings (in assorted sizes)

Elastic adhesive plasters (various sizes)
Open weave bandages 1 in., 1½ in. and 2 in. (2.54, 3.81 and 5.08 cm)
Crepe bandage, 3 in. (7.62 cm) with safety pin
Piece of sheet or headscarf
Dettol
Paracetamol (as painkiller)
Thermometer
Surgical spirit (for treating blisters, not for sterilising)

Whenever any items in the first aid kit are used, remember to replace them as soon as possible. It is a good idea to have the clearly written telephone number of your doctor, and hospital, stuck to the inside of the lid—as well as a reminder of how to telephone the emergency services. Dial 999 for the ambulance and fire services in Britain.

WHAT YOU SHOULD DO

'First aid' means just what it says. It is *first* aid, given to a victim to preserve life and prevent injuries from becoming worse. Except with minor injuries, first aid will not be sufficient in itself—second (further) aid and treatment will be required and must be sought.

The immediate treatment and attention you give includes making victims as comfortable as possible, easing pain and reassuring them. The actual action you take, and the treatment you apply, depends on the nature of the type of injury and accident.

PULSE

In an emergency it is important to be able to find the pulse—this can be felt in many places, but the most suitable ones, those that can be located quickly without wasting time, are

1 The front of the wrist (over the radial artery). About two finger widths above the crease of the wrist on the palm and the thumb side.
2 The carotid pulse, situated at the side of the neck below the angle of the jaw, at the Adam's apple level.

The pulse should be felt with two fingertips over the artery. It should be pressed gently, not hard, just enough to feel the beats.

The normal adult rate is about 60–80 beats per minute, the average being 72. This increases during exercise, and during **Shock** it will be over 100 beats per minute and may eventually reach about 150.

The normal resting rate is much higher in infants and young children.

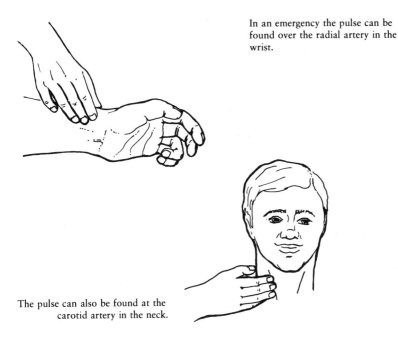

In an emergency the pulse can be found over the radial artery in the wrist.

The pulse can also be found at the carotid artery in the neck.

The average rate for a new-born baby is about 120. For a two-year-old child it is 100, and for a seven-year-old it is 90.

The quickest way of working out the rate of beats of the pulse is to count the pulse beats during 30 seconds and then multiply by two.

It pays to practise feeling the pulse on your own wrist and neck—then on others—so you will know exactly where to find these pulse positions without wasting time if an emergency arises.

EXPIRED AIR RESUSCITATION (E.A.R.)

ARTIFICIAL RESPIRATION— MOUTH TO MOUTH *and*
MOUTH TO NOSE METHOD

Breathing and heart beat may cease after **Choking, Suffocation, Drowning, Electric Shocks, Heart Attacks, Strokes, Poisoning** (including carbon monoxide poisoning) and **Unconsciousness.**

If the victim is not breathing you have four minutes in which to save a life before the brain is damaged. Some of this time may already have elapsed.

TREATMENT

1 Waste no time. Lay victim on their back and kneel by victim's side. Loosen tight clothing at neck, chest and waist. Clear any foreign matter out of the mouth with your fingers, including dentures or damaged teeth. Make sure the tongue is forward.

Expired Air Resuscitation (artificial respiration) mouth to mouth method—showing correct positioning of victim's head.

2 Place hand under victim's neck to support it, and arch it upwards, then tilt back the head with your other hand (to stop the tongue blocking the airway in the throat)—press the victim's chin upwards and open the mouth.

Press chin upwards prior to opening victim's mouth.

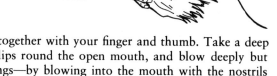

3 Pinch the nostrils together with your finger and thumb. Take a deep breath, seal your lips round the open mouth, and blow deeply but gently into the lungs—by blowing into the mouth with the nostrils pinched closed.

Pinch nostrils and blow into open mouth.

4 After the initial breath, turn your head as you lift your mouth off, so that you can observe the falling of the victim's chest as it empties.

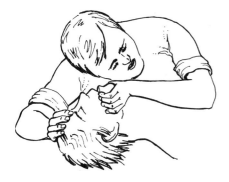

First aider lifting his mouth off and turning his head after the initial breath, to observe falling of the victim's chest as it empties.

5 Continue at a steady rhythm with one breath from you and one from the victim (still keeping victim's nostrils closed each time). Always turn your head as you lift your mouth, to watch the rise of the victim's chest to see that air is entering the lungs. Blow in again as soon as the chest has fallen.

For adults—blow once every five seconds. Continue until natural breathing is well established.

For small children and babies—place your mouth over the *nose and mouth* and give four inflations as quickly as possible. Then continue with shallow breaths every three seconds.

Use gentle blowing for children and light puffs for babies. This avoids damage to their delicate lung tissues.

For small children and babies the first aider's mouth should be sealed over the child's nose and mouth during the inflations. Use gentle blowing with children, and light puffs with babies—this avoids damage to their delicate lung tissues.

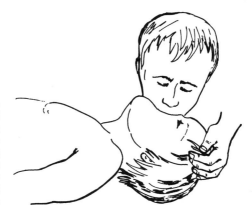

6 Continue for as long as necessary, until victim's colour has improved and breathing is completely restored. Close observation must be continued and maintained.

7 If they are not injured put them in the **Recovery Position** until medical assistance in the form of a doctor or ambulance has arrived. Do not go for assistance first, start the artificial respiration immediately, and continue it until successful, before calling for help.
If someone else is with you—get them to call for an ambulance while you start the artificial respiration.

8 If the respiration is unsuccessful after the first quick breaths—check the mouth in case the airway is re-blocked, then re-extend the neck into the approved position and start the resuscitation again.
Continue until breathing is restored.

9 If the victim vomits, immediately turn victim's head to one side to let vomit escape. Clean out any vomit remaining in their mouth—then resume resuscitation.

10 If the victim is an adult or older child and you are unable to open the mouth, or it has an intractable blockage, or your mouth is too small to form a seal over and round the victim's mouth—use the *mouth to nose* technique.
Keep the victim's lips firmly shut using your fingers or thumb to hold the lower jaw. Breathe into the victim's nose with your mouth sealed round the nostrils.
Continue with the recommended rate of blowing once every five seconds (with your mouth sealed round the nostrils and keeping victim's lips closed) until definite breathing is restored.

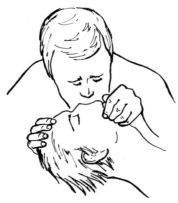

Mouth to nose method. Holding the victim's jaw to close victim's mouth, first aider breathes into the victim's nose.

11 No matter how well victims may appear to have recovered—they must *always* be sent to hospital.

12 *Note:* In some instances, breathing may cease or heart beat may stop, in others instances, both conditions can occur *together*. Victims who are not breathing are usually a blue-grey colour. In cases such as asphyxia they are usually blue-grey whether there is a pulse or not. If the blue-grey colour increases in spite of **Expired Air Resuscitation (E.A.R.)**—or you can feel no pulse—**External Cardiac Massage (E.C.M.)** must be given immediately to save the victim's life.

EXTERNAL CARDIAC MASSAGE (E.C.M.)

If the heart stops beating, the oxygen provided by the artificial methods of resuscitation will not reach the brain tissues, and the victim will die unless heart massage is given to stimulate the heart back into action.

It is essential to make sure the heart has really stopped, as it can be very harmful, possibly fatal, to give massage to a heart which is still beating. (This is why E.C.M. should never be practised on any individual— only on the special anatomical model of the body used by medical and first aid organisations.)

HOW TO CHECK IF THE HEART HAS STOPPED

In addition to the visible symptoms—the blue-grey colour (or cherry-pink skin colour in certain cases of carbon monoxide poisoning), and widely dilated pupils—the quickest way to check if the heart is beating while carrying out artificial resuscitation is to check the *carotid* pulse. This is situated on either side of the neck just below the angle of the jaw, at the Adam's apple level.

Place two fingertips over the *carotid* artery. Gently, not hard, just enough to feel any beats. If there is no pulse there, the heart has stopped beating.

TREATMENT

1 Put the victim flat on their back on the ground—with head bent back into the position for **Expired Air Resuscitation.** When heart massage is needed, artificial respiration will also be required.
The surface must be firm and unyielding.

2 Kneel beside the victim and give three firm slaps over the lower half of the breastbone. This may re-start the heart beating.

3 If there is no response, start **External Cardiac Massage** while continu-
ing to ventilate the lungs—in the ratio of one inflation of the lungs
to five compressions of the breastbone.

Put the heel of one hand on the lower half of the breastbone—with
the *palm and fingers raised* from the victim's chest.

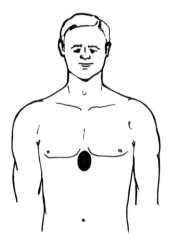

External Cardiac Massage. Pressure site
point on lower half of breastbone.

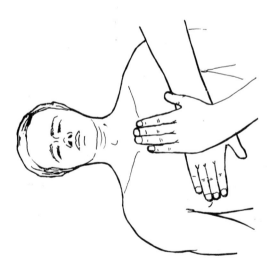

Correct positioning and
placing of hands.

4 Cover the heel of this hand with the heel of your other hand and rock
your body forward with straight arms and press down on the lower
half of the breastbone with a firm but controlled pressure. This should
move the breastbone about 1 to 1½ in. inwards (2·54 to 3·81 cm).
Violent action can break ribs.

Rock your body backwards a little to release the victim's chest, letting
the breastbone rise automatically to its normal level—keeping your
hands in position.

The forward movement should be quicker than the recovery movement.

For adults—repeat the pressure once every second.

For children—increase the rate to 60—80 times per minute. Reduce
the pressure by using *one hand only*.

For babies—increase the rate to 100 times per minute. Reduce the
pressure by using *fingertips only* instead of rocking with your hand,
and raise the position on which you push to the *middle* rather than
the *lower* point of the *breastbone*. This will reduce the risk of damage
to the ribs and liver which are particularly vulnerable in small babies.

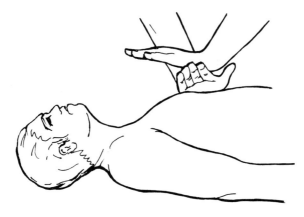

The heel of one hand on the lower half of the breastbone—with the palm and fingers *raised*
from the victim's chest.

5 *Artificial respiration will always be needed at the same time as heart
massage.*

Expired Air Resuscitation and **External Cardiac Massage** can be
carried out by one person but it is very hard work—so if anyone is
with you get them to help.

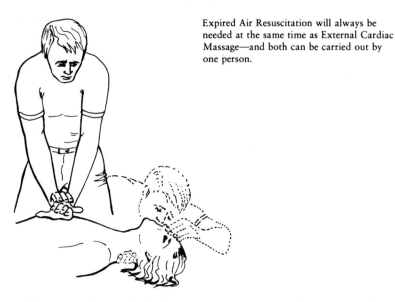

Expired Air Resuscitation will always be needed at the same time as External Cardiac Massage—and both can be carried out by one person.

If you are alone—do five heart compressions and then one mouth to mouth breath.

If there is someone with you to help—one of you should do the external cardiac massage, and the other should undertake the inflation of the lungs and feel for the pulsation of the *carotid* artery in the neck. There should be a rate of five heart compressions to one long breath of respiration.

If assistance is available—one person should do the External Cardiac Massage and the other should undertake the inflation of the lungs.
External Cardiac Massage must only be used when the heart has stopped beating. It can be fatal if carried out when the heart is still beating.

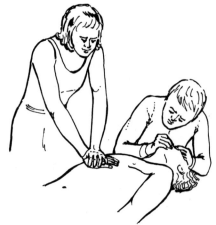

6 Check for effectiveness by seeing if the victim's colour improves—note if the pupil size has become smaller—and feel the *carotid* pulse which will become apparent with each compression.

7 Continue with the combined lung/heart resuscitation until the victim's heart beat and pulse returns spontaneously, and they breathe freely—then put victim in the **Recovery Position** until the ambulance arrives. If necessary, continue the lung/heart resuscitation until the ambulance arrives.

Victims can be kept alive in this way for at least an hour—for several hours in some cases that have been recorded.

8 *Note:* remember, **External Cardiac Massage** must *only* be used *when the heart has stopped beating.* It can be dangerous, and possibly fatal, if carried out when the heart is still beating.

The method requires skill, particularly when being carried out on the very old or very young—and it is not unusual for ribs to be cracked or fractured. However if the heart has stopped beating, the victim will die—so the risk is justifiable.

FIRST AID COURSES

Artificial respiration (mouth to mouth—and mouth to nose) **Expired Air Resuscitation** and **External Cardiac Massage** are vital to the saving of life. When needed, every second counts, and it is important to know how they should be carried out *before* an emergency arises, so that time will not be wasted.

Read the step-by-step instructions, and study the illustrations so that you know exactly what to do and how to do it. Reread this section until you know the precise routines by heart.

Then ask yourself at regular intervals throughout each year if you can still remember what to do. If you cannot, refer to the text and illustrations to refresh your memory. You must *always be ready* for any emergency, with a precise knowledge of what to do.

Ideally, join one of the short courses run by the local branches of first aid organisations throughout the world. Obtain the addresses from the telephone directory, your doctor, or local welfare organisations.

These courses, which are becoming more and more popular, are run by

THE ST. JOHN AMBULANCE ASSOCIATION (in England and Wales)

THE ST. ANDREW'S AMBULANCE ASSOCIATION (Scotland)
THE RED CROSS SOCIETY (worldwide)

The courses are held at convenient times during the day and evenings, and they are informative, easy to understand and extremely interesting. You will be shown what to do and will have the opportunity to practise first aid. In the case of E.A.R. and E.C.M. this will be done on an anatomical dummy of a body. The model reacts realistically, like a human being, without being in danger from damage caused by any lack of skill, incorrect movements or actions.

Thousands of lives have been saved by people who have been on these courses. Countless injuries have been treated successfully and prevented from developing into more serious ones.

One woman went to a first aid lecture out of *curiosity* and saved her husband's life a short while afterwards when he had a coronary attack—through knowing exactly what action she should take.

RECOVERY POSITION

Kneel beside the victim and place the victim lying on one side, with the arm and leg of the side they are lying on stretched out behind them. Remember to loosen any tight clothing around the neck, chest and waist.

Bend the other arm and leg up in front of the victim with the hip, knee and elbow almost at right angles to the body.

Turn the victim's head to that same side, and tilt it slightly backwards.

The recovery position prevents an unconscious victim from falling into a face-down position—and ensures that vomit, or anything else, will drain out of the victim's mouth and not go into the lungs—thus eliminating the chance of asphyxia.

Recovery position.

UNCONSCIOUSNESS

TREATMENT

1 Get someone to call the ambulance.

2 If breathing has stopped—quickly check the mouth and use fingers to remove dentures or loose teeth. Clear anything in mouth, including mucus, saliva or blood, with fingers or a handkerchief.

3 Immediately give artificial respiration (mouth to mouth or mouth to nose) **Expired Air Resuscitation.**

4 If heart has stopped—apply **External Cardiac Massage.**

5 Search for and control any bleeding.

6 Place victim gently in **Recovery Position** (when breathing properly and heart beating again), to allow vomit to drain naturally without obstructing the air passage.
Stay with them.
If you suspect major fractures—keep victim lying down and do not move victim more than is absolutely necessary to save victim's life. Otherwise severe and permanent injury could arise.
Make sure the victim's head is turned to one side to prevent choking in case they vomit.

7 Loosen tight clothing about neck, chest and waist.

8 Keep the victim warm—placing one blanket or rug over them.

9 Do not try to give the victim anything to eat or drink while the victim is unconscious.

10 Any victim who has lost consciousness, even if only for a few seconds, should be seen by a doctor—even if the victim says he/she feels fine.

SHOCK

Shock needs particular attention as it can kill the victim—it is as dangerous as the injury from which the victim is suffering.

Shock arises from an insufficient supply of blood to the brain, resulting in oxygen deficiency, and can be expected in all cases of serious injury, such as, severe bleeding, severe fractures and lacerations, burns and heart attacks.

The whole aim of the first aid treatment is to lessen the shock, reassure the victim and make the victim comfortable.

SYMPTOMS

The victim's skin will be pale and cold and clammy, with profuse sweating. The pulse will be fast and weak. Breathing shallow, rapid or irregular. Speech and reactions are likely to be slow. Movement may become restless—with the victim frightened or apprehensive.

TREATMENT

1 Control bleeding or look for the cause of shock.

2 Loosen any tight clothing around the neck, chest and waist.

3 Make the victim comfortable. Preferably lying down with the head low and turned to one side. Raise the victim's legs, providing there is no injury to the legs, pelvis or spine. Move as little as possible.

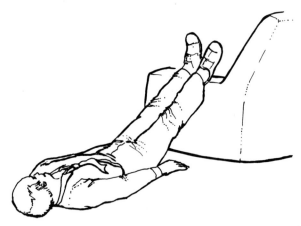

Shock can be expected after many accidents—and it can kill. The correct first aid treatment is to lessen the shock, make the victim comfortable and reassure them. Call for an ambulance in serious cases.

4 Keep the victim warm—cover victim with *one* light blanket or rug. No extra heat is needed. Maintain the body's temperature, but do not raise it. The idea is to protect, not over-heat, as too much heat attracts the blood to the skin and away from the brain and lungs, worsening the shock.

5 Reassure them constantly.

6 Do not give the victim anything to eat or drink, even if the victim is conscious.

7 Call for an ambulance.

BLEEDING

The average adult has about 6 litres (10 pints) of blood circulating in the body. This is pumped out of the heart under pressure through the arteries, and returns to the heart through veins. If veins or arteries are cut or torn—severe bleeding can occur, putting life at risk. An emergency call should be made for an ambulance.

The urgent aim of first aid treatment, in the meantime, is to stop the bleeding, or at least control it.

TREATMENT—EXTERNAL BLEEDING

1 Uncontrolled bleeding can be very frightening and you will need to reassure the victim. Act promptly, and get victim into a relaxed position.

Make the victim lie down to prevent fainting, with their legs raised, and the injured area raised if possible (unless a fracture or broken bone is suspected) to reduce the loss of blood.

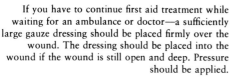

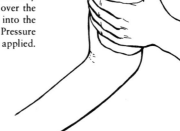

If you have to continue first aid treatment while waiting for an ambulance or doctor—a sufficiently large gauze dressing should be placed firmly over the wound. The dressing should be placed into the wound if the wound is still open and deep. Pressure should be applied.

2 Quickly apply direct pressure to the bleeding point, over a dressing, or, if the wound is large, use fingers and thumb to press the sides of the wound firmly but gently together.

You may not have time to wash your hands first if the injury is a serious one in which seconds count, and you may have to continue the pressure, and hold the wound closed, for five to ten minutes before a clot forms to close the breach in the blood vessel.

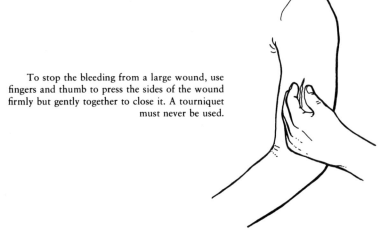

To stop the bleeding from a large wound, use fingers and thumb to press the sides of the wound firmly but gently together to close it. A tourniquet must never be used.

3 By this time an ambulance or doctor will probably have arrived and you can hand over to a specialist. But if you have to continue the first aid treatment, press a sufficiently large gauze dressing firmly over the wound, or into the wound if it is still open and deep.

Place a pad of soft material over the dressing, then secure it with a bandage.

The victim should remain lying down, and if the bleeding continues do not remove the blood-soaked dressing. Some clotting may have taken place, so put a second dressing and pad over the first, and bandage more firmly.

A tourniquet must never be used as these can be very dangerous—having led to gangrene and the loss of limbs in the past.

4 If a large foreign body is in the wound and cannot be removed—apply a light dressing that will not press the foreign body into the wound. Gauze pads can be built up around the wound, in the form of a ring, to a height sufficient to enable the dressing and a subsequent bandage

to be applied. This avoids putting pressure on the projecting foreign body.

BLEEDING FROM PALM OF HAND

1 As the hand is richly supplied with blood vessels, bleeding from the palm of the hand may be severe. After applying a dressing to cover the wound, give the victim a rolled crepe bandage to clench in the hand. This should provide the necessary pressure to control the bleeding.

Uncontrolled bleeding can be very frightening. In extreme cases it can put life at risk. It must be treated immediately—with direct pressure being applied to control the bleeding.

2 The clenched fist should then be firmly bandaged and kept elevated to the shoulder-line.

TREATMENT—INTERNAL BLEEDING

1 An ambulance must be summoned immediately, as the victim will need urgent admission to hospital.

2 If conscious, the victim should be made as comfortable as possible, preferably lying down.
If this is not possible, the head and shoulders should be raised.
Tight clothing should be loosened, and nothing given to eat or drink.

3 The **Recovery Position** must be used if the victim is vomiting or unconscious.

4 The only first aid treatment suitable for internal bleeding, while awaiting an ambulance and medical help, is that for **Shock.**

CHOKING

Choking can happen to people of all ages. Mostly it occurs through choking on food. Obvious ways of preventing such accidents are to cut up food, especially meat, into smaller portions, and to eat more slowly and chew more thoroughly before swallowing.

Choking can happen when the windpipe is blocked by a slipped denture, or by food or vomit 'going down the wrong way', or when a small object such as a child's toy obstructs the passage of air into the lungs.

TREATMENT

1 If the victim is coughing and spluttering but appears healthy, do not interfere. This is nature's way of helping.

If you can, reassure the victim by telling them to try to breathe slowly and deeply—this sometimes helps relax the windpipe muscles and leads to the release of the obstructing object.

2 If the victim is coughing and struggling for breath, or the object is obviously firmly lodged in the throat, the victim will become pale or blue in the face, limp and will soon be unconscious.

If the victim cannot breathe, there are only four minutes in which to save a life—so you will have to act fast.

3 A quick attempt should be made to remove any obvious obstruction from the mouth or back of the throat. If you are unsuccessful or cannot find anything—

4 **Immediately** dislodge the obstruction in the windpipe with a series of quick hard blows between the shoulder blades, with the victim held in the following positions

Babies

Hold babies upside down by their ankles, securely so they cannot fall, and give them a firm slap three or four times between the shoulder blades.

Toddlers

Put an older child head downwards over your knee, and give three or four quick hard blows between the shoulder blades.

Adults

Bend them forward, and give three or four hard blows between the shoulder blades—but much more vigorously.

To dislodge an obstruction in the windpipe of a choking baby give the child three or four quick slaps between the shoulder blades.
Toddlers should be positioned head downwards over your knee.

Choking adults should be bent forward and given three or four hard blows between the shoulder blades.

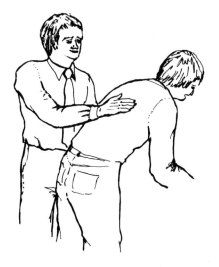

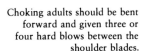

5 If unsuccessful and the choking is severe get someone to call the ambulance—and immediately proceed with the **Abdominal Thrust.**
To do this, first put the victim upright on his/her feet and grasp round the waist from behind.
Then clench one fist with the thumb-side towards victim's stomach and clasp the fist with the other hand. The fist should be above the navel and below the rib cage.

If a blow between the shoulder blades is unsuccessful and the choking is severe immediately proceed with the Abdominal Thrust—and send someone to call an ambulance. This method must be used only if all other methods have failed.

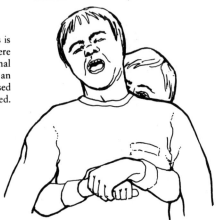

Give a sudden squeeze, pushing the clenched fist as far as possible into the upper stomach with a lifting thrusting motion. The piece of food or other obstructing object should shoot out after one or more hugs.

The victim should be taken to a doctor for a check-up as soon as possible.

6 If neither of these procedures work, and the victim is limp and blue—start mouth to mouth or mouth to nose **Expired Air Resuscitation E.A.R.**

If you are alone, stay with the victim and remain with them. Give E.A.R. immediately. Firm slow blowing sometimes enables air to get past the blockage, and enables the victim to survive until specialist medical help arrives. The chance of blowing the obstruction or foreign body deeper is a very small one.

7 **Expired Air Resuscitation** should be given to adult or infant victims who have difficulty in breathing after any obstruction has been expelled.

8 *Note:* the 'blows between the shoulder blades' method should always be adopted *before* attempting the **Abdominal Thrust** manoeuvre. There have been one or two cases where the spleen has been ruptured with the **Abdominal Thrust** technique, but, as with all emergencies if one first aid method fails, i.e. the blow between the shoulder blades, then another should be tried. The **Abdominal Thrust** is worth trying where a life would otherwise be lost. Possible injury is obviously

better than almost certain death, and the **Abdominal Thrust** method has been used successfully in many thousands of cases throughout the world; this method should *never be practised* on a normal healthy individual.

SWALLOWED OBJECTS

If small round objects are swallowed into the stomach without causing obstruction, breathing difficulties or injury to the throat, no immediate first aid treatment is necessary. This applies to adults and children. The objects usually pass through the intestines without trouble within a few days. Laxatives should not be given.

If the victim experiences pain, or the swallowed object is straight rather than round or has a sharp end (such as pins, needles, open safety-pins, fish bones, bone splinters, etc.), contact your doctor immediately for medical advice.

ASPHYXIA (SUFFOCATION)

Asphyxia is anything which prevents the lungs from receiving a sufficient supply of fresh air, depriving important organs in the body, especially the brain, of oxygen.

Unless action is taken immediately, the result will be a loss of consciousness. And if the condition continues, a failure of the heart action and death.

Apart from obstructions to breathing caused by **Choking—Suffocation** at home is usually caused by things like plastic bags, or by a cushion over the face, or from bedclothes or airtight plastic materials falling over the face while the victim is in bed, cot or pram. A baby lying face downwards on a soft pillow can suffocate as can a child swallowing the fluff from woollen materials. Overlaying (accidental smothering) can occur to an infant who is in an adult's bed.

Alternatively, if an unconscious person is lying on his/her back, there is the possibility of the tongue falling back and blocking the airway. Asphyxia can also arise from other causes (see **Poisoning** section—poisoning by gases).

TREATMENT
1 If the brain is deprived of oxygen for more than four minutes there

will be permanent damage. Speed is therefore vital. Particularly as some of this time may already have elapsed.

2 Remove any obvious obstructions.

3 Start (mouth to mouth or mouth to nose) **Expired Air Resuscitation** immediately.

4 If the heart has stopped beating—or stops beating—also give **External Cardiac Massage.**

5 If the victim remains unconscious after heart beats and breathing are restored—place the victim in the **Recovery Position.**

6 Call for an ambulance.

7 If the victim is conscious, and breathing, and their heart is beating, place them in the **Recovery Position** and seek medical advice—or get the victim to hospital.

DROWNING

Speed is vital when saving anyone from drowning, and time must not be wasted trying to force water out of the victim's lungs. The amount of water that gets into the lungs is normally minimal, and if the victim is not breathing you have only four minutes in which to save the victim's life before the brain is damaged. Some of this time may already have elapsed so **Expired Air Resuscitation** must be started at once to get oxygen into the victim's lungs.

TREATMENT

1 Quickly check for any obstruction of the mouth and back of the throat. Look for such things as weeds, stones, mud, leaves or false teeth, and remove these as quickly as possible as soon as you have got the victim out of the water. Then make sure the tongue is forward and is not blocking the air passage.

2 If the victim is still not breathing, mouth to mouth or mouth to nose **Expired Air Resuscitation** must be started at once.

3 If the heart has stopped, attempts must be made to start it beating and assist circulation. This involves **Expired Air Resuscitation** and **External Cardiac Massage.**

4 Your whole attention should be directed towards saving the victim's

life. Get someone to call an ambulance if you can but if you are alone, see to victim and then, when successful, send for an ambulance. The victim will require medical aid, a check-up and skilled observation.

5 When successful in restoring breathing and heart beat, place the victim in the **Recovery Position** while waiting for the ambulance and medical help. The victim may vomit. Any remaining water not expelled automatically from the victim's body during E.A.R. or E.C.M. will probably drain out of the victim's mouth when the victim is placed correctly in the **Recovery Position**.

ELECTRIC SHOCK

SHOCKS FROM DOMESTIC SUPPLY
Electric shock from a low-voltage domestic supply may stop heart and breathing. It can cause severe burns or prove fatal. Every second counts as the longer the victim is in contact with the current the worse the chance of survival.

TREATMENT

1 Switch off the current at the socket and remove the plug, in situations where there is no switch at the socket—remove the plug, or turn off the mains supply at the fuse box. Do whichever is easiest and quickest.

2 If this is not possible, the victim must be removed from the electrical contact. But *on no account touch the victim or a live appliance with your hands or any other part of your body*—otherwise the shock will pass through you and you could be badly burnt or electrocuted.

Never touch the victim of an electric shock until the current has been switched off. If you are unable to switch off at the socket or mains, this illustration shows a safe way to move an appliance away from a victim still in contact with the electrical current.

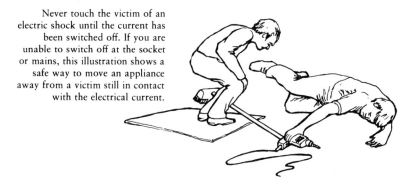

Stand on some *dry* insulating material (such as wood, newspaper, rubber mat or sheeting), and use a wooden chair, stick, broom handle, folded newspaper, rubber or other non-conductive and non-metallic object, or dry clothing to pull or push the victim clear of the electric wire and appliance. Or pull or push the appliance away from the victim, but do not touch it yourself. An umbrella should not be used as it contains metal shafts.

3 Electric shock often shows little external damage. So check immediately to see if the victim is breathing and if the heart is beating, and apply mouth to mouth or mouth to nose **Expired Air Resuscitation** and **External Cardiac Massage** if necessary.

4 If there are burns treat as outlined under **Burns and Scalds.**

5 In either, or all, of these events, the victim should always receive medical attention following first aid.

SHOCKS FROM HIGH VOLTAGE OVERHEAD CABLES

Contact with high voltage overhead cables can be fatal; or can cause serious injury, including severe burns. Alternatively, sudden muscle spasm may throw the victims away from the point of contact, and result in serious injuries from a fall. In cases where the spasm affects the muscles of the chest, asphyxia may result.

TREATMENT

1 If the victim is still in contact with, or close to, a high voltage current— do not touch or attempt to rescue them. Otherwise you could become a victim yourself.
Normally safe insulating materials, such as wood, are no longer safe for moving a victim as the high voltages can jump considerable gaps and can also cause flash burns.

2 No approach should be made towards a pylon or pole carrying electricity, or a caravan television aerial or a boat mast, or a kite or model aeroplane in contact with an overhead line, until the current has been cut off.
Everyone must be kept at least 20 yards (18 metres) away while an emergency call is made to the police (dial 999 in Britain). They will contact the electricity authority and get them to cut off the current.

3 When it has been established that the current has been cut off, and kept off, the appropriate first aid treatment should be carried out immediately.

The treatment will depend on the type of accident and the state of the victim.

See under

Expired Air Resuscitation (mouth to mouth or mouth to nose)
External Cardiac Massage
Falls
Burns and Scalds
General Shock

4 In most parts of Britain, when a call is made to the police asking them to contact the electricity authority to cut off the supply they put a call through to the ambulance service as well. In any event, and in any country, make a point of asking for an ambulance. The victim will need second, and further medical aid, after your first aid treatment.

FALL INJURIES

The most common injuries to occur as a result of falls are fractures, dislocations, strains and sprains.

A *fracture* is a broken bone. Common sites are fractures of the arm, ankle, collar bone, foot, jaw, leg, neck, pelvis, rib, skull, shoulder, spinal cord and thigh.

Closed or simple fractures are where there is no wound leading down to the broken bone.

Complicated fractures are those which penetrate the skin or other organs. These are serious, and will be associated with a general degree of **Shock.**

Dislocation refers to the displacement of a bone at a joint. Common sites for dislocation are the lower jaw, shoulder, elbow, thumb and fingers.

Strains arise through the overstretching of muscles.

Sprains are more serious, as they result from the wrenching or tearing of ligaments and tissues connected with and supporting a joint. The shoulder, knee joint and ankle joint are common sites.

TREATMENT

1 Never move the victim of a fall unless it is absolutely necessary. Fractures, dislocations, strains and sprains are not always easy to detect, they often require X-rays at hospital before diagnosis can be

certain, and movement could cause severe injury and irreparable damage or handicap.

2 Control any severe bleeding immediately.

3 Cover any wound with a dressing, and bandage lightly. Do not attempt to push any bone back into position.

4 Get a doctor or ambulance as soon as possible.

5 Treat for **Shock** if necessary.

6 Cover the victim with a blanket or rug.

7 Give no food or drink in the case of a serious fracture, as there could be internal injury and the victim may need an anaesthetic.

HEAD INJURIES AND CONCUSSION

These require expert help and should be seen by a doctor. If possible the victim should be transported by ambulance.

BURNS AND SCALDS

Burns in the home are usually caused by fire, flame, heat, electric current and corrosive chemicals. *Scalds* by boiling water, steam, spilt hot drinks and hot fat.

All burns and scalds should be regarded as serious, even those which appear relatively minor as they can run deep, with damage to the under-lying tissue.

TREATMENT

1 Clothing saturated with boiling water or hot liquid should be removed carefully but immediately.
Burnt clothing (or material) which has cooled and is still adhering to the wound should not be removed, as this could cause unneccessary pain and the material will have been rendered sterile by the heat.

2 Blisters should not be punctured or drained.

3 The affected area should be placed under slowly running cold water,

or immersed in cold water, and kept there for at least 10 minutes (or as long as necessary) until it can be removed without pain recurring. Restrictions such as rings and bracelets should be removed (with the water making this easier by acting as a lubricant) in case swelling develops.

4 If it is not possible to immerse a burnt or scalded area, such as the head or the whole body, a continuous supply of towels soaked in cold water should be applied.

5 The burn or scald should afterwards be covered with a dry sterile dressing. Do not use oil, cream, lotions or ointments.

6 Normal household chemical burns should be treated in the same way; use copious amounts of water to dilute and wash off the corrosives.

7 Severe burns, however caused, should receive prompt hospital attention once the initial first aid cooling down treatment has been carried out.

8 If the victim is conscious, water may be given to drink every 10 minutes. Only give small amounts, which must be sipped, otherwise there could be a risk of vomiting.

9 Reassure the victim at all stages, as being burnt or scalded is a frightening and painful experience. In most cases the victim will need treatment for **Shock**.

10 In the case of minor burns and scalds the same first aid treatment should be followed, and a doctor should be consulted if a large area of skin is involved.

POISONING

POISONING BY MOUTH
Medicines and drugs in liquid, pill or tablet form, chemicals and cleaning fluids, petrol and paraffin, weedkillers, fungi and plants and berries are among the poisons frequently swallowed by accident.

TREATMENT

1 If the victim is not breathing, but their heart is still beating, immediately start mouth to mouth or mouth to nose **Expired Air Resuscitation**.

2 If there is no response and the heart stops beating, commence **External Cardiac Massage** as well.

3 If the victim is unconscious, but breathing, put the victim in the **Recovery Position**.

4 Call for the ambulance in all cases—and state that the victim is suffering from poisoning.

5 If the victim is conscious try to find out what they have taken. Do this immediately, as they may soon lose consciousness. If the victim is a child take the remaining pills or container with you to the hospital, so the contents can be positively identified. Any samples of vomit may also help in the diagnosis.

6 In all cases stay with the victim until the ambulance or medical help arrives. The victim may appear to have recovered but may have a convulsion, be sick, lose consciousness, collapse or suddenly stop breathing.

FOOD POISONING
Staphylococcal and *Salmonella* are two types of common food poisoning (mentioned in the chapter on *Hygiene in the Home*).

The *Staphylococcal* symptoms are abdominal pains, nausea, vomiting and diarrhoea, and they usually make themselves felt within a few hours.

The symptoms for *Salmonella* are similar, but are not usually felt for about twelve hours. They may be accompanied by sweating, cramps and shivering, and a headache.

TREATMENT

1 The treatment in both cases should be to rest the victim in bed, with no solids being given—until the doctor comes.

POISONING BY GASES
This can occur from breathing town gas (sometimes referred to as manufactured gas). It can also result from breathing carbon monoxide which is present in the exhaust fumes from petrol engines, or from wood, coal or charcoal fires, or from faulty oil burners and other appliances requiring oxygen for combustion, where there is insufficient or poor ventilation. Even the fumes from bonfires can prove dangerous if inhaled.

TREATMENT

1 First aid treatment calls for cool thinking and prompt action.
The victim must be moved from the poison gas source and taken into fresh air, but the rescue must be done carefully, otherwise you could be poisoned. Carbon monoxide gas is colourless and odourless, and can kill without warning.
Take a couple of deep breaths, then crawl or bend down as low as possible and hold your breath for as long as you can, while you go in to make the rescue. Drag the victim out into the fresh air.
If you are unable to do this in one go, and if there is a window, open the window and get the victim to it. Take a couple of deep breaths of the air, hold your breath, then open all windows and doors.

2 When safely out in the fresh air, loosen the victim's clothing and, if they are not breathing or if their breathing is irregular, begin **Expired Air Resuscitation.** Use **External Cardiac Massage** if the heart stops or has stopped beating.

3 If the victim is breathing but unconscious put them in the **Recovery Position.**

4 Call for an ambulance.

5 If the victim is conscious, use the relevant treatments for **Shock.** Always seek medical advice or get the victim to hospital.

CUTS

TREATMENT

1 Clean the skin around the wound with cold water, making sure you wash *away* from the wound and never towards it.

2 If the wound is a small one, it can be cleansed under the cold tap provided that the water comes direct from the mains supply.

3 Cover the wound with a gauze dressing and secure it with a bandage or adhesive tape. If the wound is still bleeding, a thick dressing will be necessary. This can be built up from a gauze/cotton wool/gauze sandwich.
The open-weave bandaging should be firm to secure it. It should not be too tight.

4 An anti-tetanus injection may be needed—and the cut may need stitching.
In any event, if there are any doubts or misgivings, seek medical advice immediately.

5 For the treatment of *major cuts*—see **Bleeding**. If a finger or toe has been severed—remember to take the finger or toe along in the ambulance. Sometimes it is possible for a surgeon to reattach them.

REMOVING SPLINTERS

1 Clean the area round the splinter with cold water before carrying out an inspection or treatment.

2 If the splinter is long, or is lodged deeply or is contaminated with soil from the garden, or is a deeply embedded thorn, the victim should be taken to a doctor who will remove the splinter and say whether an anti-tetanus injection is required.

3 Other splinters can be removed with a needle. Dip this in Dettol—make sure the needle is perfectly clean—then put it in neat antiseptic or boiling water.

4 The needle can then be used to loosen the skin round the splinter, then use eyebrow tweezers (treated in the same way as the needle before use) to remove the splinter.
The wound may bleed slightly and this should be encouraged by squeezing gently round the wound. Apply a sterile dressing and secure it with an adhesive plaster or bandage.

5 If the victim feels pain some time afterwards, the wound should be inspected to make sure it is healing normally. If not, get medical advice.

EYE INJURIES

TREATMENT OF FOREIGN BODY IN EYE

1 Injured eyes must never be rubbed.

2 To remove foreign bodies from the eye—wash your hands and sit the victim under good light, facing you. Examine the eye, then its eyelids.

Pull down the lower lid while the victim looks up, then raise the upper lid and ask the victim to lean their head back slightly and to look down. If the speck is visible on the eyelid or on the white of the eye, try to remove it with the soft fold of a clean handkerchief or a wisp of cotton wool—moistened with clean water and shaped to a point.

Removing a foreign body from the eye. In more serious cases, or where something is embedded in the surface of the eye, treatment must be carried out by a doctor.

3 If this is unsuccessful, fill a basin or bowl of clean water and get the victim to blink the eye under water as this often removes the foreign body.

4 If the damage appears serious, or something is embedded in the surface of the eye, the treatment must be carried out by a doctor. If this is out of surgery hours, or your doctor is out on his or her rounds, the victim should be taken straight to the hospital for treatment.

TREATMENT OF CORROSIVE CHEMICALS IN EYE

1 Chemical accidents can be serious, and swift action is vital to prevent permanent scarring, damage or loss of sight.

2 If cleaning fluids, or any other household or garden chemicals are splashed or get into the eye, the answer is to immediately flush out the eye. Dilute the chemical with lots of clean water.
If both eyes are affected, get the victim to blink repeatedly under clean water.

3 Alternatively, if only one eye is affected, sit the victim down with their head tilted back and turned towards the injured side.
Be sure to protect the undamaged eye, then flush the injured eye,

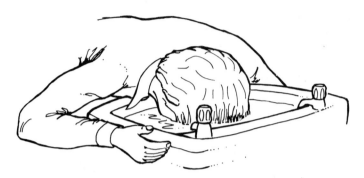

Foreign bodies can be removed from the eyes by blinking them repeatedly under clean water in a basin or bowl. This method helps prevent the scarring, damage and loss of sight that can occur if household or garden chemicals have been splashed into the eyes.

gently but continuously, with a flow of water from a clean cup or jug so that it runs across the surface of the eye—flowing into one corner and out of the other.

4 It is vital to remove any chemical trapped under the eyelids, so the eyelids must be held gently open with the fingers of your free hand. The flushing operation will need to be repeated for some time, possibly for 10 minutes, and certainly until the affected eye is thoroughly cleansed.

5 If necessary an eye pad may be put on, or a dressing lightly bandaged over the eye. Take the victim straight to hospital. The doctors will give the eye a thorough medical examination and will carry out any further treatment which might be considered necessary.

HEART ATTACKS

Although a heart attack does not really come under the heading of an accident – it does come under the more general heading of *Safety in the Home*. Each year many thousands of lives could be saved if people learned how to recognise the symptoms of a coronary attack, contacted a doctor immediately—and knew how to carry out the correct first aid.

In Britain many lives are lost, or put at risk unnecessarily, through delay in calling a doctor. People either do not recognise the symptoms, or if they do, they imagine the symptoms will go. In other cases people do not like to call out their doctor in the middle of the night. Speed is essential. In the United States, after a coronary campaign was given wide publicity, the average delay in calling a doctor was cut by half.

The victim may or may not have a previous history of chest pain—ask the relatives.

SYMPTOMS

The pain usually starts in the middle of the chest, building up steadily in intensity, often radiating to the neck area and down the arms, more usually the left arm. The pain is not a stabbing one, it is tight and vice-like and it may also be felt in the back between the shoulder blades.

Additional symptoms are shortness of breath, cold sweating, and a weak pulse which may also be irregular. The victim will have a slate-grey colour and lips may be bluish—there may be nausea or vomiting, or the victim may empty their bowels or feel as though they need to.

Any chest pain with a cold sweat should be regarded suspiciously.

TREATMENT

The major aim of first aid is to reduce the work of the heart and sustain the victim during an attack.

1 *If the heart is beating* do not move the victim. Get the victim in a semi-recumbent position with the head and shoulders raised on pillows; or propped up in bed if the victim was already there at the time of the attack.

2 Loosen any tight clothing round the neck, chest and waist. Do not give the victim anything to drink, remain calm, reassure the victim and send for a doctor immediately.

3 *If the victim is not breathing*, start mouth to mouth or mouth to nose **Expired Air Resuscitation.**

4 *If the heart has stopped beating* – make absolutely certain that it has stopped, before applying **External Cardiac Massage.** Checking this is vital, as giving massage to a heart which is still beating, in the circumstances of a heart attack, is potentially dangerous. If the heart has stopped beating, and you are certain beyond doubt that it has, then you will need to give **External Cardiac Massage**, otherwise the victim will die, unless the heart re-starts of its own accord.

5 You should call for an ambulance and medical help immediately, whenever a heart attack is suspected.

If possible, get someone to call the ambulance for you, so that you can remain with the victim. However, if you are alone, your attention must be devoted to ensuring that the victim is breathing and that the heart is beating – and that it continues to do so. When satisfied, call for the ambulance, then return to the victim.

STROKES

These are caused either by bleeding, from a ruptured blood vessel into the brain, or clotting which cuts off the supply in a blood vessel to the section of brain served by that vessel.

Both cases deprive the brain tissue of vital oxygen.

SYMPTOMS
The symptoms and results of a stroke vary considerably. They depend on the extent of the damage and the part of the brain affected. There may be a sudden loss of movement, power or sensation in a limb—or slurred speech—or complete loss of consciousness. Look for drooping of the mouth and eye on one side of the face.

The victim is very often unconscious—but breathing, though of a laboured nature.

TREATMENT
1 Call for an ambulance or a doctor.
2 Do not give the victim anything to eat or drink in case their swallowing muscles have been damaged.

HYPOTHERMIA

SYMPTOMS
Hypothermia is due to severe accidental cooling of the body and may occur at any age. It affects the elderly living in unheated rooms or homes. They may also be on an inadequate diet. Hypothermia is very common with the aged after a fall when the femur (thigh-bone) has been injured and the victim has been on the floor all night.

Hypothermia should be suspected if you find an elderly person in extreme conditions of cold, appearing pale, confused and in a state of collapse or unconsciousness.

The victim will feel very cold to the touch, their pulse is likely to be slow and weak and hardly noticeable at all, and their breathing will be slow and short. The extreme lowering of the body temperature is dangerous, and if their temperature is below 35°C (95°F), the lowest scale on a normal thermometer, the victim is suffering from hypothermia.

TREATMENT

1 If the victim is unconscious, call for an ambulance and give first aid treatment as described for **Unconsciousness.**

2 If they are conscious (or unconscious), the aim must be to prevent further heat loss and improve the body heat and circulation.

3 The victim should be placed between blankets, positioned *loosely* around them (or over them if in bed). *On no account use hot-water-bottles or electric blankets.*
The rewarming process must be slow and gradual otherwise sudden reheating can cause heart failure and be fatal.
If possible, the room should be warmed. Be careful to keep heaters away from beds, furnishings and anything else that might catch fire.

4 If the victim is conscious, then warm (but not hot) sweet drinks can be given provided they are taken *slowly.*

5 In either case, whether you are treating an unconscious or conscious victim, a call must be made for an ambulance as soon as you can, as the *gradual* rewarming process requires specialist medical skills and facilities.